HISTORY IS WATCHING:

HOW DO WE RESPOND TO TRUMP?

JOHN WRIGHT

RAINY CITY PUBLISHING

Rainy City Publishing
P.O. Box 82813
Kenmore, Washington 98028
Copyright © 2019 By John Wright
All Rights Reserved
Second Edition 2019

ISBN 978-1-79669-412-3

To my grandparents and step-grandparents,

John, Edith and Arthur
Darwin (Tim), Myrtle and Oliver

whose wisdom and love motivated me
to think, to aim skyward and grasp my dreams

CONTENTS

CONTENTS

ACKNOWLEDGMENTS

MY PARENTS, RICHARD AND HELEN, gave me the freedom to satisfy my curiosity by meandering my own winding path as I saw fit, while teaching me honorable conduct by example.

Maria is the love of my life who gave me the greatest joy, Juliana and Joseph. Juliana and her husband Tyler made me a joyful grandfather with Grace. My in-laws, José and Juliana, influenced many people, including me, by leading principled and dignified lives. I am proud of the accomplishments of my niece Marcella.

My brothers Rick and Stephan and sisters Roxane and Cathy provide insight and companionship.

Peter Muello sacrificed his free time to diligently and wisely shape an ungainly manuscript into a readable book. For that I am deeply and humbly grateful.

John Wright
Seattle
March 2019

"And ye shall know the truth, and the truth shall make you free"

– John 8:32

AUTHOR'S NOTE

WHEN DONALD TRUMP claimed the presidency after the November 8, 2016 election, I was forlorn, as were millions of other people. It was not a matter of being a sore loser. After all, the candidate I supported got 48.2 percent of the popular vote, or 2,864,974 more votes than Trump's 46.1 percent.

I was worried that it doomed democracy as we know it. Trump showed a shocking absence of knowledge about how the government works and an even more disturbing lack of interest in learning what he did not know. He spewed out vicious lies every day, attacked everyday citizens, and his followers seemed oblivious to the harm he causes. From the start, Trump and the people in his administration seemed to corrupt everything around them.

And it wasn't just Trump. Before he took office, Republican appointees on the Supreme Court showed an inclination to sanction gerrymandering and voter suppression. States in which citizens were split nearly 50-50 in votes for Congress were undemocratically skewed toward the Republicans: 13-5 in Pennsylvania, 9-5 in Michigan, 12-4 in Ohio, and 10-3 in North Carolina. District boundaries were cynically designed to pack all the Democrats into a few districts and spread Republican voters into more districts they could win by smaller margins. States enacted all sorts of rules solely to prevent Democrats from voting: moving polling stations to places with difficult access, requiring forms of ID that many people did not have, scrubbing people from voting lists if they had not voted in the last election or if their name and birthdate matched someone in another state, hours-long lines at polling places in Democratic-leaning areas and no lines where Republicans could breeze in and out, and shortening voting hours (See Chapter 3).

The Citizens United Supreme Court ruling opened the floodgates for special interests to make secret unlimited contributions for attack ads, letting them buy candidates and overturn good-government reforms that sought to clean up campaign financing.

Putting together these factors and more, it seemed that the voices of voters were snuffed out by the rich, powerful and corrupt; the future of our nation looked bleak.

I'd seen this playbook before, and it was profoundly chilling. I lived in Venezuela during the eighties, when the vibrant multiparty democracy was the envy of Latin America, then watched in horror two decades later when Hugo Chavez destroyed the institutions which guaranteed democracy and imposed dictatorial rule. So, when Trump came to power, I feared it was already too late in the United States, that he had inflicted the same mortal wounds to the American experience and that while retaining the veneer of democracy, we were inevitably careening down the same dead end.

Then came the 2018 midyear elections, and American citizens, enraged by Trump's actions and the widening morass, returned Democrats to a majority in the House of Representatives while taking back a good number of governorships and state legislative seats.

Crucially, this expression of democracy in its purest form gave Democrats the constitutional and statutory authority to investigate Trump and his cronies after Republicans for two years failed to provide even a fig leaf of oversight.

The purpose of this book is not to convince Trump supporters of the facts. Unfortunately, they believe what he says. Like Stepford wives, they unquestioningly accept what Fox News and other right-wing propaganda bullhorns tell them. This book has three motives: First, as a clearinghouse for cataloguing the most egregious offenses by Trump and his minions which are hurled at us so fast and furious that it's impossible to keep track. Second, historical perspective. I am convinced that if people consider how their children and grandchildren will one day look at today's events, many of them will realize what an unworthy legacy we are bestowing. Third, a call to action. Chapter 8, "Solutions: A Plan of Action" provides a roadmap for engaged citizens to reverse the damage. The outcome is not clear. We could wake up in a year or two to find that the American experiment in democracy has vanished. We can't let that happen. Only by concerted, unified action can we prevent our nation from following the same path toward autocracy as Venezuela, Turkey, the Philippines and other nations which were democracies in the recent past.

AUTHOR'S NOTE

There are more of us than there are of them. Trump's approval rating has always been underwater. We must start washing the Trump stain from our national conscience immediately. When our grandchildren learn about Trump and ask us what we did to stop him, do we want to say that we voted for him or that we sat on our hands while he desecrated our finest traditions? Or will we honestly be able to say that we worked hard through democratic means to restore national unity and greatness?

Act now. Our own future most certainly depends on it.

Because many people will probably read this book on subways, trains, buses and airplanes, rather than curled up in their favorite cozy chair, the printer made the typeface a little bigger for easier reading in imperfect surroundings. Confession: I often read on public transportation, and it is always challenging. I hope everyone has an easy, enjoyable and enlightening reading experience.

PREFACE

The Origins of Trump's Candidacy and His Support

It is better to be feared than loved

–Niccolò Machiavelli

DONALD TRUMP didn't burst on the scene all at once. He had been a celebrity much of his life as a flamboyant real estate developer, TV personality and playboy. He was a media creation, frequently asked for his opinion about public issues despite the fact that he seemed to know little about much of anything. He hobnobbed with the rich and famous, and political donations bought him access to the power elites. He even contributed to Hillary Clinton's campaign for Senate in New York.

He flirted with the idea of running for president for years, and there was occasional chatter that he might become a candidate. But nobody really took him seriously, that is, except The Donald himself.

No one thought Trump would last long when he entered the race in June 2015 by riding down an escalator in Trump Tower to make his announcement in front of actors, all of them white, paid fifty dollars apiece to cheer. More than a dozen big-name Republicans were running, and the odds-on favorite was

Jeb Bush, the former Florida governor with great name recognition, mainstream views, a winning smile, political experience and family pedigree: the grandson of a senator, son of one president and brother of another.

The field had some legitimate heavyweights. There was Ohio Governor John Kasich, Texas Senator Ted Cruz, Florida Senator Marco Rubio, former Virginia Governor Jim Gilmore, New Jersey Governor Chris Christie, former Pennsylvania Senator Rick Santorum, Kentucky Senator Rand Paul, former New York Governor George Pataki, South Carolina Senator Lindsey Graham, Louisiana Governor Bobby Jindal, Wisconsin Governor Scott Walker and Texas Governor Rick Perry. All had applicable political experience.

The pundits were dumbfounded when the big names fared so poorly in primaries, caucuses or debates and flamed out faster than shooting stars. Trump roared through the primaries and kept winning even as he committed a series of blunders. It was always assumed that the next screw-up would end his meteoric rise as quickly as it began. After all, quirky outsider candidates such as Herman Cain and Ben Carson shot up in the polls for a short while, then flamed out when it became obvious that they weren't fit for the job. Trump appeared fated for the same "fifteen minutes of fame" before the inevitable implosion.

If the infamous "Access Hollywood" recording of Trump bragging about sexually molesting women didn't knock him off track, what else would? There were rumors of a "pee tape" involving Russian prostitutes urinating for him, but it never saw the light of day. A seemingly endless parade of women came forward to accuse him of sexual misconduct. Numerous reports surfaced about questionable business deals and even possible links to organized crime. There were hints of Russian ties, but most of what we know now came out after the election. Trump University, which closed its doors in 2010, was sued for fraud by those who attended the seminars. Reporters dug into four bankruptcies declared by Trump's companies to avoid paying creditors. The Federal Trade Commission fined Trump for antitrust violations involving his casinos in Atlantic City. Contractors sued Trump for nonpayment. Former models for Trump Model Management sued the agency for not getting them proper work visas. Contestants at his beauty pageants accused him of barging into their dressing rooms while they were undressed. The nonprofit Trump Foundation, rather than doing charitable work, instead paid personal expenses for things like settling Trump's legal disputes and later was shut down.

Any one of these events would have jettisoned a normal candidate. But Trump is anything but normal. Trump and his factotums described the lawsuits as a routine "cost of doing business." Really? Numerous members of my family and close friends have owned a wide variety of businesses; none of them has ever been sued.

Trump became the vessel for many grievances. People on the lower rungs of the economic ladder were increasingly frustrated about declining living standards as the few at the top kept pulling further ahead. Some white people thought minorities had more privileges. Religious conservatives were told that Christians are persecuted. Trump became the vehicle to register their protest, especially when his Republican rivals embodied the resented establishment. Many people were fed up with the government's inability to get things done, a feeling that insiders controlled everything amid favoritism for elites. They were convinced that "Crooked Hillary" had gamed the system and that it was time to "drain the swamp." How would supporters of Trump, the purported outsider, have reacted if they knew before the election that Trump instructed his personal lawyer, Michael Cohen, to bribe people to rig public opinion polls? Irrespective of ideology, Trump spouted out so much spellbinding malarkey that he was seen as an agent of change who would shake things up, while Hillary was viewed as a perennial insider who offered more of the same. Polls showed a surprising 12 percent of voters who had backed Bernie Sanders, who calls himself a democratic socialist, chose Trump instead of Hillary.

After he won, many people, even foes, hoped for the good of the country that Trump would grow into the job, that he would end the rhetorical excesses and be willing to learn from experts about how to carry out his unique responsibilities. But, over and over, it was obvious that he makes up his mind before the facts are in, refuses to study issues in depth, has little curiosity, and is so thin-skinned that he constantly taunts anyone who refuses to march in his lemming parade. His only concern is keeping a moat around his narrow, shrinking base. These details are gleaned from revelations by his former associates and allies, not his critics.

After all that has happened, most astounding is how nearly all elected Republicans willingly prostrate themselves before the Emperor With No Clothes. And equally incredible is how, after two years of a Trump presidency, close to 40 percent of the population cling to him despite all the staggering, incontrovertible disclosures of wrongdoing on so many levels. It seems as if they all have "Stockholm syndrome," a psychological phenomenon in which hostages feel empathy for and sometimes identify with their captors.

Trump's detractors don't give each other high-fives in congratulations that they called it right. Instead, people of all political stripes are increasingly frightened that he may do something terribly wrong that will permanently damage our security or freedom. By early 2019, two children in custody had died, as well as numerous adults, amid his "zero tolerance" policy toward immigrants. Millions of people worry that even worse tragedies await us around the next bend. So much could go wrong: Trump grovels before dictators, savages relations with traditional allies, mocks solidarity with NATO members and even questions whether we should belong to NATO at all, while reversing decades and even centuries of consistent foreign policy.

My goal is not to bash Trump and his followers. Rather, it is to serve as a call to action to preserve our democratic traditions through education and peaceful activity. I ask everyone to look ten, twenty, thirty or even fifty years into the future and try to picture Trump's legacy by then. One thing is certain: we will all be collectively judged by history and by our descendants. Did we strengthen or weaken American democracy and our place in the world? Were we on the right side of history or the wrong side?

INTRODUCTION

From "God is Watching Us" to History is Watching

I personally believe that those who are leaders with political power over the world will be forced some day, sooner or later, to give way to common sense and the will of the people
–Alva Myrdal

SOME RELIGIOUS PEOPLE use phrases such as "God is watching" as a warning that just because people get away with wrongdoing today, they won't in the long run because God is the final arbiter of right and wrong. Religious or not, everyone can use this as guideline for their own behavior. If you prefer, think of history as watching us individually and collectively.

For the prominent, especially, the whole world is watching. Bill Cosby went from being America's favorite dad a generation ago to the butt of jokes, spending his golden years in prison instead of a mansion after conviction for numerous sexual assaults.

A comedian recently said that if you asked people years ago to choose, between Donald Trump and Bill Cosby, which one would some day be president and which one would be in prison for sexual misconduct, the overwhelming response would have been the opposite of what fate delivered us. One was a celebrity playboy and serial adulterer and the other admired for family values. Cosby has fallen from grace, but the other side of that equation remains open.

Historians will judge us tomorrow – Americans as a whole, our political leaders, and President Trump himself – based on what we do today.

For perspective, think of the shadow that hung over Germans long after Hitler. Why did they allow a once-enlightened nation to inflict the world's greatest horror upon so many people? Why didn't they rise up and stop the madness? We ask why our own ancestors didn't treat Native Americans better or demask the Ku Klux Klan instead of silently letting them lynch people for the color of their skin.

Similarly, our descendants will most certainly demand to know why we let Trump trample on our traditions and laws. What will you tell your granddaughter when she asks, "Grandma, what did YOU do when Donald Trump took babies away from refugee mothers? Did you try to stop it?" When climate change causes fires, floods and famine, will you tell her you believed Trump when he ridiculed global warming as a hoax?

If your grandchildren are born into a nation and world far less free than the one you grew up in due to Trump's depredations, will you admit your role in doing away with the good old days? This is not conjecture or hyperbole. It is happening today, every day, as Trump erodes the ties that bind us together, intentionally divides us by pandering to a narrow, hateful base, and ignores fundamental precepts of America.

It's do or die. It's now or never. We must all stand with one clear voice insisting that this is wrong. America is – or was – too good to be ruined by an egomaniac who cares only about himself.

History is Watching: How Do We Respond to Trump? offers a brief look back at history for context, and in the end I offer some simple options for restoring traditional American values before it is too late.

History is unblinking, and the results are often murky. History will evaluate us based on our words and deeds today. We have to be brutally honest about the shortcomings of our own past before we preach to others. When we look back at our forefathers, we are grateful that their legacy to us was a Constitution that guarantees liberty for all Americans. But didn't they also condone slavery? Don't we all recognize that basic flaw in their thinking? Thomas Jefferson was considered a great president, albeit one with a blemish: his mistress was the slave Sally Hemings. Does that change our opinion of Jefferson the man, apart from Jefferson the president and founding father? We have overthrown democratically elected governments in Guatemala, Iran and other nations, then propped up merciless dictators when it suited our interests. We have invaded nations that posed no legitimate threat to us.

We need to learn from the past, avoid the same mistakes, and do better tomorrow. As the landscape changes day by day, we must react to new events. When Trump intentionally separated children from refugees, who raised their voices against this barbaric practice? Americans found it

INTRODUCTION

unconscionable when Stalin snatched children from parents in the Soviet Union, yet they are willing to accept their own president doing the same thing? Climate scientists almost universally believe that human activity causes global warming, and most Americans agree. Yet we still allow Trump to favor polluters, withdraw from the Paris Accords and give away national monuments to energy companies who donate heavily to Republican campaigns? Americans believe safety regulations are important, but Trump wants to dismantle the Chemical Safety Board, which inspects chemical plants and oil refineries. Do we really want to invite more industrial tragedies?

I was raised by hardworking parents. My father sold insurance, earning an honest living by finding the best policies for customers. When a competitor forced him out of business by bribing the head of a business association, my dad did not become bitter or stoop to the same trickery. He regrouped and started a new business along with my mother. This was the best example possible for their children. My dad's father, who served in the Michigan legislature in the 1940s, hired a black office assistant and was criticized by fellow state senators. My mom's father was a social worker during the Great Depression. When he came home from work, he would ask my grandmother to make extra food so he could deliver it to the troubled families he met. Later, as the world confronted the horror of the Holocaust, my father, his brothers and my grandfather all joined the military to fight fascism. Further back, my ancestors served in the Revolutionary and Civil Wars to create and then preserve the United States.

I'm proud of my heritage and I hope to make my children and grandchildren proud of me some day. Many families surely have similar stories. So how do we explain to our children and grandchildren that we stood by a president who was so overtly dishonest? Trump built housing that discriminated against tenants by race. He cheated contractors out of their wages. He declared bankruptcy whenever it suited him, clutching his own assets while leaving his small business subcontractors in ruins. We don't teach our children to conduct business that way, so how can we condone it from our president?

My motives are not partisan. I am a Democrat, but I have worked on campaigns for both Democrats and Republicans. I have voted for Republicans, independents and minor party candidates when I believed them to be the best candidates. If John McCain or Mitt Romney had become president instead of Barack Obama, I would not be outraged. Both men had the judgment and character to serve as president and lead our nation honorably. I may have differed with them on specific policies, probably quite often, but I would not condemn them morally. McCain served our country admirably, as both a soldier and senator. Only Trump says "he is not a hero." Romney may have been clairvoyant when he said in 2012 that Vladimir Putin's Russia was the greatest foreign policy challenge to the United States at a time most Americans were understandably more fearful of Al-Qaeda and ISIS terrorism. After democratic reforms by Mikhail Gorbachev and Boris

Yeltsin, and before Putin invaded Ukraine and annexed Crimea, we were relieved to hope that Russia could qualify as a friend after decades of Cold War hostility. In hindsight, Romney obviously called that one right.

This is my fourth book. I have been aghast at Trump's behavior for decades, but I fought the impulse to write about him, thinking that everybody sees the harm he is doing and that his fans will never listen to reason. Why bother? I decided to propose a new approach, a roadmap out of the quicksand.

My earlier books always endeavored to distinguish lies from the truth. *The Obama Haters* focused on the smears and slurs against the then-president and showed the facts behind the slander. The second book, written together with scientist Steve Hallett, *Life Without Oil*, dealt with the misinformation about carbon-based energy and the real-world complications of the transition to new energy sources. More recently, *Lost & Found in Latin America*, sought to dispel common misconceptions about that culturally rich and diverse region extending from the Rio Grande to Tierra del Fuego.

That brings me to this book. It is a clarion call for Americans to become aware, demand the truth and take peaceful, democratic action to restore our birthright. Trump is not the cause of all these problems. He is a symptom of an ongoing campaign to hijack our democracy to serve the interests of a powerful few, of the influence of money on our public discourse and life, and of a willingness by many people to follow forceful leaders who march us to ruin. Such leaders are called demagogues. It's nearly impossible to convince their followers of the truth. Luckily, they are a minority of the population. We must sidestep those who allow themselves to be misled and instead take our message to those already alarmed by Trump but who don't know what to do or what action to take, and to those in the middle who sense something is wrong. Let's get to work.

1

THE GRAND SWEEP OF HISTORY, AND WHY IT MATTERS

Those who don't know history are doomed to repeat it
–Edmund Burke

W E ALL JUDGE OUR FOREBEARS, both positively and negatively, with the advantage of hindsight. We thank our founding fathers for bestowing a Constitution that guarantees our freedom even as we continue to debate those rights and responsibilities regarding religion, free speech, ownership of lethal weapons, and countless other issues.

Yet we feel shame that those same forefathers accepted, and even embraced, slavery as an institution. They allowed other human beings to be shackled, brutalized and dehumanized, even while paradoxically calling themselves democratic and Christian. Today it seems inconceivable that they were blind to such obvious injustice.

Some of the earliest works of historical analysis examine the decline and fall of the Roman Empire, the world's greatest and most enduring of the ancient states. It lasted for a millennium, encompassing much of Europe, the British Isles, North Africa and a large swath of the Middle East. For centuries, historians have sifted through the records, and they remain deeply divided on the topic.

In the late eighteenth century, Englishman Edward Gibbon wrote what was then considered the definitive account, a six-volume narrative. He posited that barbarians overcame Roman defenses due to a loss of morality among the citizens.

While there is little dispute that invasions by Germanic tribes signaled the end, the empire had been crumbling for more than a century. The economy faltered amid military overspending and a dwindling supply of slaves. Wealthy citizens fled and established their own fiefdoms, eroding the tax base. The vast territory was difficult to govern and hard to protect from invaders. Corruption flourished and eroded central control. The arrival of Christianity in 313 dispelled the belief that the emperor was divine. Roman citizens were reluctant to become soldiers, forcing the government to hire mercenaries whose loyalty could be bought by a competitor offering better perks.

Today, speculation on Rome's downfall ranges from the advent of Christianity to corruption, economic inequality and militarism. In *Life Without Oil*, Steve Hallett and I hypothesized that a shortage of fuel hastened the end. The Romans burned wood, and trees got scarcer the closer you came to the center of Roman civilization because they were not being replanted. In other words, Rome was an early example of environmental degradation. What we most remember from history was the moral decline of its rulers, from Caligula to Nero.

Why do we care? Because we want to avoid the errors of the past that could affect us the same way. The study of great societies that flourished and collapsed can draw useful, if disturbing, parallels. We have to examine where Trump fits into our history of leaders. We must candidly observe the present, look toward the future and remain mindful of the past. We need to strengthen America and our democracy, or risk falling prey to the same weaknesses that felled earlier, more enduring and even greater empires.

2

HOW ONE BAD LEADER CAN
DESTABILIZE DEMOCRACY

*If you wish the sympathy of the broad masses,
you must tell them the crudest and most stupid things*

–Adolf Hitler

EXAMPLES OF FAILED STATES ARE ALL AROUND us. They can be found in every region of the world and period of history. Most were never successful, robust democracies. They were always hobbled by poverty, corruption, lack of basic institutions to guarantee basic liberties, and citizens unwilling or unable to change the status quo.

Then there are the true democracies that slid into dictatorship and chaos and others which turned to autocratic rule, such as Turkey, Hungary and Poland. And we can't forget early twentieth-century Germany.

Mustafa Kemal Ataturk founded modern Turkey a century ago, a wisp of the former Ottoman Empire that once proudly spanned southeastern Europe, the Middle East and northern Africa. While most countries with Muslim majorities were theocratic, Ataturk applied his own blueprint. He forged a secular nation which modernized, became prosperous, and allied itself economically, politically and militarily with the West. This formula worked for nearly a century, with many of the freedoms enjoyed by Western nations. But in recent years, as radical Islam has rocked the region, President Recep Tayyip Erdogan has moved steadily toward authoritarian rule, chipping away at democratic traditions and exploiting religious fundamentalism as relations sour with long-time allies in the North Atlantic Treaty Organization, known as NATO. Despite these alarming trends, Donald Trump expresses only admiration for Erdogan.

Hungary and Poland were part of the Soviet bloc, secured by the Soviet military's brute force for four decades from the end of the Second World War until 1989. As the Warsaw Pact disintegrated, both countries joined NATO and the European Union. Both had become stable democracies until their elected leaders began to flout democratic norms and veered toward autocracy.

Even Russia briefly flirted with freedom under the leadership of Mikhail Gorbachev and Boris Yeltsin. But Vladimir Putin rolled back the glasnost, and his monocratic rule today echoes of the czars.

Latin America is rife with countries that have yo-yoed between democracy and dictatorships of the right and left. The most glaring example is Venezuela, a collapsed state governed by inept, dictatorial kleptocrats that was until recently an enduring democracy, Latin America's shining star. In the 1980s, Venezuela brokered peace talks for its warring Central American neighbors. It provided low-cost oil and refined fuels at a discount to impoverished neighbors reeling under high prices after OPEC embargoes sent prices soaring. It welcomed refugees from military dictatorships across the continent, in particular, educated professionals from Argentina, Chile and Uruguay who fled persecution or death at the hands of ruthless military juntas.

Newly arrived in Venezuela in early 1981 as a foreign correspondent, I thought it was election season because the political rhetoric coming from all sides was so heated, employing colorful invectives. It was a fun, carnivalesque atmosphere that everybody got in on. I soon realized that the next elections were nearly three years away, in December 1983. But their democracy was so buoyant and infectious that it resembled what America might be if it were born in the tropics. After all, the national hero in much of Latin America is Caracas-born Simon Bolivar, who has a monument with his likeness in every city in Venezuela as well as statues throughout the hemisphere, including New York's Central Park. Bolivar used the United States as the template for his homeland. When I got there, marches to protest every imaginable cause erupted regularly, snarling traffic and making the loud city even noisier, but they almost never got out of hand as people lived and breathed a vibrant democracy. Corruption was widespread but tolerated because everybody, even those living in the precarious *ranchos* clinging to hillsides, had enough to eat, a roof over their heads and access to free education.

Oil income trickled down to all *Venezolanos*. Gasoline cost mere pennies per gallon, keeping bus fares cheap and allowing many working class people to drive full-size, locally manufactured American-brand cars. The middle class was thriving, and the rich were fat and happy. Bright students earned *becas*, scholarships to study abroad, most of them in the United States. They returned home equipped to work in the oil industry or professions such as law, medicine, dentistry or business management. When the government nationalized the oil companies in 1976, these were not expropriations like in Cuba. Rather, Venezuela bought out the foreign companies such as Standard Oil, Mobil and Royal Dutch Shell and made them subsidiaries of Petroleos de Venezuela (PDVSA), while keeping their employees. As Americans and Europeans returned home or retired, they were replaced by qualified Venezuelans. PDVSA was a model for other developing nations to take control of their own resources in an orderly way without making enemies of the foreign companies that built their industries.

The ruling party regularly got thrown out every five years, and the opposition roared back in. The winners took the spoils, and minimal effort went into training an effective, impartial civil service. But all was not well. Resentment seethed just beneath the surface. People earning low wages resented well-paid PDVSA employees. Of course, the catch was that those employees were highly skilled. But that did not stop the envy. Along came a savior to exploit those fears and resentments against the entrenched PDVSA "elites." Sound familiar?

Hugo Chavez, a former military officer who had previously been jailed for attempting a coup, was elected president in 1998 and took office in early 1999. Stoking underclass discontent, he raided the PDVSA piggy bank, leaving less funding for capital-intensive oil projects to maintain the business. After a general strike in late 2002 and early 2003, Chavez fired anyone believed to sympathize with the strikers and replaced them with political loyalists, up and down the line. People with years of experience were dismissed, and their replacements were poorly trained. PDVSA's entire brain trust disappeared. Chavez demanded foreign partners make huge investments, and when they balked, he grabbed their property. But the seized assets and equipment were worthless if not properly operated and maintained, so drilling rigs and heavy machinery sat idle, rusting. Before Chavez, Venezuela was one of the world's most prodigious oil exporters, and it also shipped refined products. Exports peaked at more than three million barrels per day in the late nineties. By early 2019, oil sales had withered to one-third of peak levels, and Venezuela was forced to import huge amounts of gasoline it could ill afford. Oil derricks and refineries were in a constant state of breakdown. If fighting corruption was a pretext to justify repression, it's a hollow excuse. As the economy crumbles, corruption gets worse.

The nation's biggest export became people, as Venezuelans from all walks of life swelled land border crossings with Brazil and Colombia while others risked their lives on any boats available to reach nearby Caribbean islands north of Venezuela, such as Trinidad, Curacao and Aruba. Venezuela's days as a regional haven are now a distant memory. Under the disastrous administration of Nicolas Maduro, who took over upon Chavez's death, at least three million Venezuelans have fled the country over the past four years. The nation has lost about 10 percent of its population, and more keep leaving every day. Some head overland to Colombia and then south to Peru, Ecuador, Chile and Argentina. Others trudge northward to Panama, Costa Rica, Mexico and the United States. This is a tragedy for an oil-rich nation that once packed its pampered middle class into jetliners for weekend shopping sprees in Miami, where their free-spending ways gave rise to the catchphrase, "It's so cheap I'll buy two."

During those times, many unskilled Colombians crossed the border to work in their oil-rich neighbor. When a Colombian committed a crime, chest-thumping Venezuelans would trumpet their outrage at the dangerous immigrants (sound familiar?). Graffiti said in big letters COLOMBIANOS FUERA (Colombians get out). In one of history's ironic turnarounds, Venezuelans have become the illegal aliens in now-stable Colombia, spurring resentment there.

Venezuela is not just another banana republic that collapsed. Those are easy to find. Venezuela was a thriving democracy, both economically and politically, a beacon to its neighbors. If Venezuela can fail in just a few short years, perhaps we could too. Our experiment with democracy has lasted longer, but history is replete with empires that crumbled. Venezuela is striking because Trump shares disturbing similarities with Chavez and Maduro: disdain for democratic traditions, egotism, an unwillingness to listen to others, divisive policy, and the treatment of adversaries as enemies.

I lived in Venezuela years before Chavez and Maduro

came to power. I also lived in Mexico and Brazil, which face mammoth challenges, from crime, corruption and poverty, but neither one is a failed state.

Don't take my word for any of this. I highly recommend a useful book, released in 2018, which studies how democracies descend into autocracy or outright dictatorship. *How Democracies Die* by Steven Levitsky and Daniel Ziblatt, professors of government at Harvard University, meticulously examines governments of the left and right that turned their backs on representative democracy. They sound a loud warning that Trump is attempting to undermine the legitimacy of elections (false allegations of massive voter fraud by illegal aliens), baselessly describes opponents as criminals ("Lock Her Up"), encourages violence, and attempts to restrict civil liberties. The authors write that democracy doesn't always end with a bang, but often with a whimper as essential institutions such as the judiciary and the press are weakened: "The good news is that there are several exit ramps on the road to authoritarianism. The bad news is that, by electing Trump, we have already passed the first one."

Levitsky-Ziblatt clearly explain in detail the dangers our democracy faces with Trump as president and our partisan divide. The authors do not delve into why Republicans have been more willing than Democrats to violate the longstanding principles that have maintained comity and good governance since the Civil War. I believe it is elemental: a craving for power. Raw and naked. We all played King of the Hill as youngsters. You pulled down whoever was on top and fought off everyone who tried to dislodge you. That is Trump's game. He is amoral and apolitical. He only values what maintains his power. He will abandon a strategy in an instant that suits his erratic whims and enhances his perception of power. His only ideology is himself.

Shortly after taking office, Trump demanded personal loyalty from the heads of federal law enforcement and security services. When FBI Director James Comey pledged fidelity to the nation rather than the president personally, Trump fired him. He attacks the FBI, Justice Department, courts and the media whenever they counter his version of events. (See Chapter 3).

Abraham Lincoln got it right back in the nineteenth century when he observed: "America will never be destroyed from the outside. If we falter and lose our freedoms, it will be because we destroyed ourselves." The examples where democracy has slipped away – Venezuela, Turkey, Poland, Hungary and others – were not attacked by enemies on the battlefield. Rather, devious leaders used the tools of democracy to exploit and widen existing fissures to inflate their powers.

American democracy can best be protected by an informed, engaged population. We must learn from the mistakes of others, as well as our own, to reclaim our heritage. Critics need to be mindful of the terminology they use. Calling Trump a dictator, Nazi or fascist is counterproductive because his supporters say simply he's no Mussolini or Stalin. A more effective line of criticism may be to point to Trump's risky tendencies that reject the precedents laid down before him, for which the examples are legion.

For example, Trump shamefully uses speeches before impartial groups like the Boy Scouts and military to deliver partisan rants and belittle political adversaries.

Perhaps the world can tolerate the loss of freedom in Venezuela, Turkey, Hungary or Poland. But the United States? Ronald Reagan's shining city on a hill? What happens when the United States is no longer the world's democratic model? What becomes the new model?

Trump's greatest foes may not be Democrats and liberals; he appears to be his own worst enemy. His greed, insensitivity and outright cruelty have turned many former friends and associates against him. Officials in top-level security posts have said they are working for the administration out of loyalty to America to protect the country from his worst tendencies. The Trump White House leaks worse than a broken sprinkler, largely out of fear by aides that his proposals and behavior could harm the country. The postscript at the end of this book quotes former members of Trump's Cabinet and other top aides condemning him.

An anonymous Trump adviser in September 2018 published an opinion piece in *The New York Times* titled "I Am Part of the Resistance Inside the Trump Administration." The official wrote that Trump faces an unparalleled test because "many of the senior officials in his own administration are working diligently from within to frustrate part of his agenda and his worst inclinations. I would know. I'm one of them." The essay explains that members of the administration want Trump to succeed "but we believe our first duty is to this country, and the president continues to act in a manner that is detrimental to the health of our republic." The author says "the root of the problem is the president's amorality" and describes him as "anti-democratic." There are "whispers within the Cabinet of invoking the Twenty-Fifth Amendment, which would start a complex process for removing the president" but the author blames us as a nation for allowing a President Trump in the first place: "The bigger concern is not what Mr. Trump has done to the presidency but rather what we as a nation have allowed him to do to us. We have sunk low with him and allowed our discourse to be stripped of civility."

Beltway guessing about the author's identity was feverish. Much of it focused on Dan Coats, director of National Intelligence, who is considered "one of the adults in the room" at the White House, in other words, a serious professional with qualifications to perform a highly sensitive job rather than a know-nothing Trump flatterer. Coats, a former Republican senator from Indiana, denied the speculation. The author's identity remains unknown.

Concern for America under Trump is especially noteworthy by independent good-government groups. "The United States retreated from its traditional role as both a champion and exemplar of democracy amid an accelerating decline in American political rights and civil liberties," the nonpartisan Freedom House's 2018 annual report said. "Democracy is in crisis. The values it embodies – particularly the right to choose leaders in free and fair elections, freedom of the press, and the rule of law – are under assault and in retreat globally."

The report described Turkey and Hungary "as sliding into authoritarian rule" while "the world's most powerful democracies are mired in seemingly intractable problems at home."

Freedom House said: "A long list of troubling developments around the world contributed to the global decline in 2017, but perhaps most striking was the accelerating withdrawal of the United States from its historical commitment to promoting and supporting democracy. The potent challenge from authoritarian regimes made the United States' abdication of its traditional role all the more important." It said the Obama administration had "continued to defend democratic ideals" but sometimes fell short, while Trump "made explicit – in both words and actions – its intention to cast off principles that have guided U.S. policy and formed the basis for American leadership over the past seven decades." It noted that Trump rarely used the word "democracy" abroad and instead "expressed feelings of admiration and even personal friendship for some of the world's most loathsome strongmen and dictators." It counts Russia and China as "the world's leading autocracies" and lamented their gains in strength during Trump's presidency, eroding democratic values worldwide.

Freedom House rates countries using methodology from the Universal Declaration of Human Rights adopted by the U.N. General Assembly in 1948. These criteria ranked the freest nations as Finland, Norway and Sweden, with Canada and the

Netherlands close behind. The United States was placed in the second of ten tiers, fifty-first out of 159 nations surveyed. By comparison, when Barack Obama was president, the United States occupied the top tier.

A key measure of leadership is how other countries view America. The United States has always prided itself on its worldwide prestige, but that has suffered a major blow since Trump came to power. A Gallup poll of citizens in 134 countries, released in January 2018, showed that under Trump, 43 percent of respondents around the world had an unfavorable view of U.S. leadership, and just 30 percent favorable. By comparison, opinions were the opposite during Obama's last year in office, when 48 percent of people worldwide approved of American leadership and 28 percent disapproved. Interestingly, the status of other major countries was virtually unchanged. Russia had a 41 percent approval rating in 2016 and 2017. Gallup measured U.S. prestige growing in only four nations: Liberia, Macedonia, Israel and Belarus. Germany, led by Angela Merkel, is now the most-respected nation in the world, with 54 percent approving around the globe and 21 percent disapproving.

In the Americas, 58 percent of people from Canada to Argentina and everywhere in-between had a low opinion of U.S. leadership under Trump, and 24 percent had a positive opinion, a stunning reversal from 49 percent positive and 27 percent negative during Obama's final year in office.

Next door, in Canada, approval for U.S. leadership plunged forty percentage points to 20 percent approval and 76

15

percent disapproval. Opinions in our southern neighbor, Mexico, dropped 28 percent. Similar declines in approval were recorded by two close democratic friends: Panama was down thirty-five percentage points and Costa Rica fell thirty-two percentage points.

Europeans disapproved of U.S. leadership by 56 percent to 25 percent in 2017, a dramatic change from 44 percent approval and 36 percent disapproval under Obama. In the United Kingdom, our closest ally for centuries, approval slumped by twenty-six percentage points: only one-third of Brits back U.S. leadership now and two-thirds oppose it.

One country bucking the trend was Russia, precisely the nation suspected of collusion with Trump's 2016 victory. A Pew Research poll showed that 53 percent of Russians gave Trump the thumbs up in 2017, compared to 11 percent for Obama the year before. Trump is more popular in Russia than at home. Maybe he was looking at these findings when he declared, "We're respected again as a nation." In Moscow, maybe.

Trump supporters can shout "America First" or "Make America Great Again" until they are hoarse, but impartial outside organizations say the nation's essential freedoms are waning. At home and abroad, most people believe America was much greater before Trump came to office. "This historic low puts the U.S.'s leadership approval rating on a par with China's and sets a new bar for disapproval," Gallup concluded. "This report reveals U.S. alliances and partnerships are at risk."

Gallup even found that a record 16 percent of Americans reported wanting to leave the country due Trump.

3

ANTI-DEMOCRATIC FORCES PAVE THE WAY FOR TRUMP

This is systematic, it's wrong, and it's anti-American

–Congresswoman Alexandria Ocasio-Cortez

IF NICCOLÒ MACHIAVELLI saw the state of the world today, he would not be surprised. His insights into power half a millennium ago described how some leaders use "any means necessary" to obtain power. Karl Marx would smile and nod in approval at how the United States and other democratic, capitalist states are getting wobbly, and he would declare this is the natural state of capitalism destroying itself.

Donald Trump didn't just arise out of thin air. Anti-democratic forces bulldozed many norms before crowning him as their leader.

Voter suppression has increased over the past decade. Right-wing Republicans, after widespread victories in congressional and state elections in 2010 set about to remake America in their own vision. It was an alliance of convenience among three wannabe totalitarian forces: theocrats, economic conservatives, and racist nationalists. They don't all necessarily agree with each other, but their interests overlap, and they are willing to tolerate the others to share the only thing that truly matters to them: power.

The Religious Right has employed every weapon in its arsenal to limit or ban abortion, birth control, sex education and gay rights. About 30 percent of the population consider themselves religious conservatives out of 75 percent of Americans who identify as Christians. Clearly, not all Christians are the type of extremists who claim that they suffer persecution. After all, how can a majority of people be oppressed?

Economic conservatives seek to increase their wealth and power over others, sometimes ruthlessly. Every time a new law helps consumers, the environment or safety, big business grumbles that it is mistreated.

Racists are willing to accept any ally, any argument that allows them inside the halls of power. Even though 96 percent of households in the top 1 percent of income are white, white supremacists shout that Caucasians are an endangered species.

This alliance of faux grievances by a minority of the population holds the keys to power. They whine whenever they don't get their way, even though most people disagree with them on nearly every major issue. This bloc knows that it can't hold power if it plays by the rules or tells the truth, so the strategy is to distort the opposition and win by any means necessary.

Trump insists, with no evidence, that five million fraudulent votes were cast in the 2016 election. Texas officials in early 2019 asserted that tens of thousands of non-citizens voted in the Lone Star state and launched a crusade to force mostly Hispanic people to prove their citizenship or be stricken from the registration lists. Despite all this noise, a Trump-ordered investigation found virtually no cases of voter fraud nationwide. This allegation is a pretext to erect roadblocks and prevent millions of Americans from exercising their right to vote. In close elections, such as the 2016 statewide races in Georgia and Florida, banning even a small percentage of opposition voters may have tilted the Republicans to narrow victories.

Obama's Justice Department went to court to fight voter suppression tricks; the Trump administration, instead, has endorsed these practices in court.

SUPREME COURT

Associate Justice Antonin Scalia was appointed to the highest court by Ronald Reagan in 1986 and was approved unanimously by the Senate. One of the most influential judges in history, he served until his death in February 2016. That gave Barack Obama the chance to nominate a justice, his third, during his final year in office. Throughout our history, numerous judges were approved by the Senate during the incumbent's last year. In fact, one of the court's greatest minds, Benjamin Cardozo, was nominated by Herbert Hoover in February 1932 before he was routed in November by Franklin D. Roosevelt. The Senate approved Cardozo unanimously. Obama knew he was on firm ground to appoint Scalia's successor, and within a month submitted the name of Merrick Garland, the chief U.S. Circuit Judge on the Court of Appeals in the District of Columbia. Obama could have nominated someone with proven liberal bona fides to please his base, but instead Garland was a moderate who easily could have been selected by a president of either party. He was even praised by conservative Utah Senator Orrin Hatch, and not a single negative comment emerged about Garland's credentials or character. However, Senate Majority Leader Mitch McConnell, instead of fulfilling his constitutional duty to let senators vote on the nomination, reversed 227 years of American tradition and refused. Garland's appointment sat in limbo for 293 days, the longest vacancy in U.S. history, until a new Congress was seated. That left the eight-member court unnecessarily deadlocked on numerous decisions for a year and allowed Trump instead to appoint Scalia's successor.

McConnell didn't only meddle with the Supreme Court. Obama left office with 108 federal court vacancies, double the number he inherited from George W. Bush, due to Senate stalling tactics. Trump filled those vacancies with judges, some with questionable credentials, who were then rubber stamped by the Senate in which McConnell had kneecapped the minority party's rights. He quashed the Democrats' customary prerogative to weigh in on whether a circuit court nominee from their home state gets a hearing, a tool the Republicans had effectively implemented frequently to torpedo qualified Obama nominees.

"Let's let the American people decide," McConnell crowed at the time, when Obama still had a year left in office. The American people did decide. In 2012, they gave Obama 51.1

percent of the popular vote and 332 electoral votes out of 538. Obama had a compelling and resounding mandate. It would be hard to argue that Trump had a greater mandate, with 46.1 percent of the popular vote, to appoint a justice a year later.

After he gave the Senate and Supreme Court a black eye, McConnell blustered: "One of my proudest moments was when I looked at Barack Obama in the eye and I said, 'Mr. President, you will not fill this Supreme Court vacancy." McConnell did grant his party a temporary boost with favorable court decisions, but his maneuver came at the expense of irredeemably staining his legacy and that of the court. Has McConnell considered that his scheme will probably be the first line in his obituary, no matter what he accomplishes in his life? It's hard to imagine how anyone who truly cares about history and democracy would willingly subvert centuries of precious tradition for shabby partisan gain. It's a fair question to ask whether the Senate and Supreme Court will ever recover and restore their democratic luster after the body blows McConnell inflicted.

GERRYMANDERING

In 2011 redistricting, Republicans found a way to fashion what they hoped would be enduring dominance in Congress, even when they fail to win a majority of votes cast. The easiest way to achieve this was to manipulate congressional district boundaries in their favor. The goal in redistricting was to cram your opponents into a few districts they win by a landslide, then redraw the lines in the remaining districts to give themselves a narrow majority. That made it difficult for the other side to gain representation proportional to their popularity. "One person, one vote" guaranteed by the Constitution becomes just a quaint concept.

Political underhandedness is nothing new. The term gerrymandering was coined in 1812 after Massachusetts Governor Elbridge Gerry redrew state senate districts to benefit his Democratic-Republican Party against the Federalists. Because one district was described as resembling a salamander, Gerry and salamander were joined and a new word was minted.

Opportunities for gerrymandering abound every ten years after the Census records population shifts that give more congressional seats to states with growing populations and takes them away from states losing residents. This allows states to redraw their lines, which can benefit one party at the expense of the other. State legislatures are notorious for setting boundaries in lopsided ways to solidify power. But it can be done in a way that is fair for all. Washington state gained a new seat from the 2010 census and empowered a four-person commission to carve up the state. Those included one Democrat and one Republican, both former office holders, and two independents. Their new map resulted in numerous swing districts and a 6-4 advantage for Democrats, reflecting the state's political inclinations.

Other states were less evenhanded. Going into the 2018 midterm elections, states in which citizens were split down the middle were unfairly skewed toward the Republicans: 13-5 in Pennsylvania, 9-5 in Michigan, 12-4 in Ohio, and 10-3 in North Carolina, where districts were carved up to favor the GOP.

Pennsylvania's Supreme Court overturned the gerrymandered map and ordered it redrawn for the election. Even though Republicans screamed foul, the new map ended up with nine Republicans and nine Democrats, in tune with the state's near-even voter loyalties. Elections in Michigan also returned to balance with seven representatives apiece from each party.

Things went differently in heavily gerrymandered Ohio, which sent a lopsided 12-4 delegation to Congress after the 2018 election. The incoming governor, Mike DeWine, used his final days as the state's attorney general to file a successful motion to toss out a lawsuit which had sought proportional redistricting. Ohio Republicans won 54 percent of the total votes for Congress but ran away with 75 percent of the sixteen seats, while Democrats, who won 46 percent of the vote, earned just 25 percent of the representation. This is exactly how autocrats are taking control in Hungary and Poland, described in Chapter 2.

VOTER SUPPRESSION

In North Carolina, it was even worse. After Democrat Mark Cooper was elected governor in 2016 with 51 percent of the vote, the state legislature ignored the people's will and stripped Cooper's authority to make appointments, along with other powers. They didn't stop there. Ballot-tampering was so brazen in the state's Ninth Congressional district that election officials tossed out the results and called a new election for September 2019. Without a final decision about the district, the GOP has nine seats in the state to the Democrats' three, highly disproportional pillage for North Carolina Republicans who won 54 percent of the vote in 2018, while Democrats took 46 percent. While Democrats and Republicans were fighting it out, Congress refused to seat a winner until the election was clarified and certified. And one has to wonder how many votes Republicans would have obtained had they not suppressed participation through a voter ID law described by a federal court as targeting black voters "with almost surgical precision," shortening voting hours, and moving polling stations in Democratic-leaning districts to out-of-the-way locations. The catalogue of North Carolina's irregularities evokes the stacked elections in Venezuela that have raised an international outcry.

Imagine how many seats in the House of Representatives would change hands nationwide if all fifty states were true democracies! Shouldn't we all want election results that truly represent the will of the American people?

Republicans are not the only violators. New Jersey Democrats are considering legislation that could gerrymander their state, and there are accusations that Democrats in Maryland gerrymandered that state's districts. National Democrats must clean up their own house if they want to claim the high road in North Carolina, Ohio, Florida, and Georgia. If not, people could dismiss their arguments on the grounds that "everybody does it" and damage the chances for free and fair elections.

Florida's gubernatorial and senatorial races in 2018 were decided by significantly less than 1 percent in both races. Even though Florida voters restored former felons' rights to vote by a two-to-one margin in a ballot initiative that year, the law in effect at that time granted the governor sole discretion to reinstate voting rights. Rick Scott, the then-governor who was running for senator, restored voting rights to only three thousand former felons during his eight years in office. His Republican predecessors, Jeb Bush and Charlie Crist, granted clemency to seventy-five thousand and one hundred fifty thousand ex-felons, respectively. Scott left more than a million Floridians without voting rights even after completing their sentences and parole or probation (those still in prison, along with people convicted of murder or sexual offenses, are not eligible under the new law). Our system of justice operates on the philosophy that incarceration allows inmates to be rehabilitated. Also, sentencing disparity has resulted in many minorities being convicted of felonies for nonviolent drug offenses or driving on a suspended license, while whites accused of similar crimes got light sentences for misdemeanors and never lost their voting rights. Before the ballot initiative, 20 percent of African-American adults in Florida were ineligible to vote. Rick Scott seemed to know that allowing a million former felons to vote again could swing the race he ended up winning by ten thousand votes out of more than eight million cast. The new law will be in effect for the next election, so Scott and his successor as governor, Ron DeSantis, who also won by a whisker, could face tough reelection prospects unless Florida Republicans concoct new voter suppression tactics.

Under the election law that was in effect when Rick Scott and DeSantis won their offices, numerous Trump insiders, including George Papadopoulos, Paul Manafort, Rick Gates, Michael Flynn and Michael Cohen would have been ineligible to vote as convicted felons. One has to wonder why Trump associates with so many criminals.

In Georgia, Republican Brian Kemp topped Democrat Stacey Abrams by a 50.2-to-48.8 percent margin in the 2018 governor's race, according to the official results. Kemp was the secretary of state, whose office was responsible for holding the election. Abrams, who had served as minority leader in the Georgia House of Representatives, was seeking to become the nation's first black female governor.

Kemp had a questionable stint as curator of Georgia's voter rolls. During his tenure, his office illegally disclosed personal information about six million voters. Kemp then defiantly refused the Obama administration's offer to help prevent hackers from falsifying votes, accusing Obama of politicizing cyber attacks.

The election was imperiled long before voters went to the polls as Kemp refused to accept the registration of fifty-three thousand new voters signed up by Abrams allies. Curiously, that is almost exactly his margin of victory. Kemp accused the New Georgia Project, an Abrams-founded group devoted to signing up minorities to vote, of fraud even though state investigators uncovered no hanky panky.

ANTI-DEMOCRATIC FORCES PAVE THE WAY FOR TRUMP

A 2017 Georgia law requires voter information to be an "exact match" with records kept by the Department of Driver Services or the Social Security Administration. If the match is not exact, the registration goes into "pending" status and applicants must provide further information to the local voting board. It might sound fair enough until you delve into the details, including minute typographical errors such as transposing a number or letter, deleting or adding a hyphen or apostrophe, an extra character or space and use of a nickname like Rick instead of Richard. Kemp defended this law as preventing voter fraud, which is not exactly rampant in Georgia, and managed to keep Abrams supporters from voting. Despite Kemp's arguments, there was only one election fraud case in Georgia in recent years, involving a local official who was acquitted after going on trial for helping a voter who did not understand how voting machines work.

A similar tale unfolded in Kansas. Kris Kobach, as secretary of state, launched numerous efforts to stifle voter turnout. In 2005, his predecessor, Ron Thornburgh, initiated Interstate Voter Crosscheck, a database software program intended to eliminate potential duplicate voters. Kobach adopted this crusade, becoming a national advocate. The program flags voters who have the same first and last names and birthdate in more than one state. It has been criticized for providing poor data security and has often been wrong, leading to voters being incorrectly stricken from registration lists. Virginia's 2013 Annual Report on List Maintenance found a 75 percent false positive among names flagged. Only four people have been charged with voter fraud as a result of Crosscheck, and none have been convicted. A study by major universities found that for every valid double voter registration purged, three hundred legitimate voters are scrubbed.

I could have been red-flagged. More than once, I have moved from one state to another and registered to vote. My first and last names are both common. If Crosscheck had been used, it might have found me on the rolls in two states and barred my name, even though I had no intention of voting twice. I'm not alone. Fourteen percent of the population moves in any given year; many of them are likely to show up on voter rolls in both their current and former address. That doesn't mean any of them intend to vote twice. Using simple methods to prevent double registration doesn't seem to have been Kobach's concern.

Trump, alleging massive voting by illegal immigrants in the 2016 election, established the Presidential Advisory Commission on Election Integrity in 2017, with Vice President Mike Pence and Kobach in charge. Their request to each state for voter information drew bipartisan backlash, with most states refusing to cooperate out of privacy and security concerns. Some members of the commission sought to investigate the real threat to our elections, Russian hacking, but Kobach ignored them. The commission ignored common sense proposals that would improve voting integrity, such as requiring paper ballots and audits as a guarantee that votes are counted correctly. The panel was disbanded six months after it was founded.

The Brennan Center for Justice studied Trump's assertion

about illegal voting and found that out of 23.5 million votes they checked, approximately thirty cases involved voting by suspected non-citizens. "Our interviews with local election administrators made clear that rampant non-citizen voting simply did not occur," the Brennan Center said.

Accusations of voter fraud are so easy to debunk. Most of the alleged fraud occurs when someone mails in an absentee ballot but dies before election day and registrars discover the name in death records. The assertion that undocumented aliens or green card holders vote in massive numbers is nonsensical because they would risk deportation. People with permanent residency want to stay, not be expelled permanently.

In fitting irony, Kobach, who became a national figure by trying to kick voters off the rolls, found himself kicked off the public payroll in Kansas when he lost the 2018 race for governor to Democrat Laura Kelly.

4

MEDIA STOOGES

Trump's Sycophantic Conduit to His Uniformed Base

The most effective way to destroy people is to deny and obliterate their own understanding of their history

–George Orwell

ONALD TRUMP probably would never have become president had it not been for a powerful propaganda machine which smeared his opponents and distorted his record to portray him as a savior to people who had given up on government. Fox News and its right-wing chorus on the Internet for years defamed the Clintons, Barack Obama and many a Democrat and liberal. Intentional misinformation and distortions over the years by Fox could fill the Library of Congress, but for the purposes of this book I will just cite some of the more glaring episodes of deceit and how they helped create the Trump era.

Media and politics have always had a love-hate relationship. Politicians need news organizations to send their message out. The rub comes when politicians realize they can't always control that message once it's out. Media figures and politicians have been interlinked since the beginning of our nation. We've seen it often in recent years:

MEDIA STOOGES

Peggy Noonan put elegant phrases in the mouth of Ronald Reagan, who had a gift for making those words come alive in magical ways. Now a columnist for *The Wall Street Journal,* she writes poignant, loving remembrances of the Gipper but pulls no punches with his successors, party affiliation notwithstanding. George Stephanopoulos went to ABC after a stint in Bill Clinton's White House. Likewise, Paul Begala and James Carville migrated to CNN after working for Clinton. Obama's media strategist David Axelrod has a show on CNN. Jenna Bush Hager, daughter of Bush the Younger, is a host on NBC's *Today Show.* Nicolle Wallace, who worked for W. as well as John McCain, expresses daily outrage about Trump's behavior on her MSNBC show. Chris Matthews, an aide to the late House Speaker Thomas "Tip" O'Neill, has been jabbing guests for more than twenty years with his sharp verbal elbows as the referee on MSNBC's *Hardball.* Chris Cuomo, son of the late New York Governor Mario Cuomo, has a show on CNN. The list goes on and on. Media people with previous political experience share rich behind-the-scenes insights into how campaigns and the White House operate.

Yet not all are equanimous and fair minded: Sean Hannity and some of his fellow travelers on Fox News are flagrant exceptions. The long-time host of a highly rated prime-time news and "information" show, Hannity has become an unpaid "adviser" to Trump via frequent telephone calls and even appeared at a Trump rally during the 2016 campaign. In fact, Hannity ranted about the "abusively biased hate-Trump media," seeming to forget that he spent years obsessively defaming Obama and the Clintons.

To the other networks and news figures mentioned previously, that would have seemed a conspicuous violation of ethics. But if many find Hannity's behavior and tirades unprincipled, he has exposed his true colors. He is proudly and brazenly part of the Trump brigade. For those who are not fans of either Trump or Fox News, Hannity has permanently branded himself with a scarlet "T" for Trump.

Hannity is not the only media big shot who nibbles on Trump's ear. Members of Congress in both political parties did something rare in late 2018: they worked together and compromised to avert a government shutdown. Trump promised to sign this legislation and even told House Speaker Nancy Pelosi and Senate Minority Leader Charles Schumer in a White House meeting that he would accept blame if the government shut down. Then radio trash talker Rush Limbaugh and columnist Ann Coulter scolded Trump. He saw that as his marching orders: shut the government down, no matter what he had promised Congress or the American people.

Limbaugh commands almost cultist devotion from his fourteen million listeners he calls "dittoheads." The U.S. population was 323 million at the end of 2018, which means that 309 million people do not listen to the rotund clown.

Hannity, Limbaugh and Coulter may all be riding high now, but history has a funny way of sorting things out. Limbaugh and Coulter are inordinately nasty toward anyone with whom they disagree.

Luckily for us, most news organizations are willing to

stand up for the truth and report honestly about the Trump administration. All presidents have a testy relationship with the media because it's their job to be the watchdog. Thomas Jefferson had tough words for newspapers. "Nothing can now be believed which is seen in a newspaper. Truth itself becomes suspicious by being put into that polluted vehicle," he said. Despite this opprobrium, our third president also defended the necessity of a free press: "The basis of our governments being the opinion of the people, the very first object should be to keep that right; and were it left to me to decide whether we should have a government without newspapers or newspapers without a government, I should not hesitate a moment to prefer the latter."

While every president since Jefferson has experienced tough sledding with the fourth estate, Trump is the first one to launch full-throated condemnations, labeling the news reports he does not like as "fake news." He has called the media the "enemy of the American people," indulging in hate-mongering and press bashing similar to Hitler, Stalin and Hugo Chavez.

Curiously, Trump himself is a media creation. In the 1980s and 1990s, his real estate and casino ups and downs were front-page fodder in the tabloids, as were his romantic dalliances. He had a prime-time TV program on NBC, *The Apprentice*, for fifteen seasons starting in 2004. And he had a sweetheart deal with the tabloid, *National Enquirer*, which thrives on celebrity scandals, the accuracy of which is always tenuous. At Trump's behest, *Enquirer* paid for exclusive interviews with women who had negative tales to tell about him, only to bury the stories. The practice, called "catch and kill," is the subject of Special Prosecutor Robert Mueller's probe. Figures linked to this practice are under indictment for concealing information about alleged illegal activity. Another Trump ally, Jerome Corsi, is being investigated by Mueller. He wrote *The Obama Nation*, which FactCheck.org described as "a mishmash of unsupported conjecture, half-truths, logical fallacies and outright falsehoods."

For more than a decade, print newspapers have been faltering as the Internet robbed them of advertising revenue (when did you last place a classified ad in a newspaper instead of Craigslist?) and readers, who largely ditched daily newspapers delivered to the door and began to "read it on the Internet." Of course, it is more convenient to read today's events on your computer or cellular telephone, and many newspapers went out of business while others struggle to remain relevant and survive. Even the venerable Associated Press, my former employer, was forced to slim down and reinvent itself. But the convenience comes with a nagging question. If we want to read news on the Internet, where will that content originate? If a news organization can't pay journalists to report the news, where will it come from? Bloggers? Many are blowhards, not reporters, who spin second-hand information. Bloggers don't do the legwork of attending committee meetings in Congress or develop sources in government offices, non-governmental organizations and businesses. Bloggers don't sift through the pros and cons, dig deep for all the facts and try to come up with a coherent version of events. That's not their job. So who is going to do that if the traditional news organizations don't have the money and staff?

Luckily, the traditional media, after doing a poor job of sorting out the cranks from the serious critics of Obama and Clintons, rose to the occasion. Granted, Trump is an easy target, but it's easy to take potshots from the sidelines. The hard work is digging for the truth. The Trump years have become the media's finest hour since the Watergate era, when intrepid footwork by dogged reporters exposed the chicanery of President Richard Nixon and his associates and ultimately brought about their downfall. Without a free and courageous press, Nixon and Vice President Spiro Agnew may have gotten away with their crimes and been outed only later by historians.

The New York Times, nicknamed the "gray lady," *The Washington Post*, now owned by Amazon.com CEO Jeff Bezos, and *The Wall Street Journal* cover Trump aggressively. *Journal* readers must feel like they have whiplash because much of its news contradicts its columnists, frequently unthinking, unapologetic drones who regurgitate right-wing spin. One columnist dismissed all of Trump's misdeeds and instead blasted Obama for "weaponizing the IRS." This was not while Obama was president. This was in 2018! This columnist was referring to the faux scandal when Republicans accused the Obama administration of using the Internal Revenue Service to harass Republican critics by requiring political attack machines to justify their nonprofit status. The IRS only denied nonprofit status to one of those political groups it investigated. Guess what? It was a liberal group. But years later, right-wing ideologues continue to dredge it up for lack of anything damning to pin on Obama. Other *Journal* columnists continue to smear Obama as corrupt. Despite investigation after tiresome investigation, nobody in the Obama administration was ever found guilty of any wrongdoing. By contrast, how many people in Trump's circle have already been indicted? Do *Journal* columnists even read the news in their own publication? Nevertheless, all three newspapers deserve applause and support for their excellent investigative work (I subscribe to all three). Fox News and the right-wing world love to call the *Times* and *Post* biased favoring liberals. Yet they quote generously from both newspapers when it suits their needs. Sure, all news organizations get it wrong sometimes. People can be misquoted and some facts may get jumbled. But it's usually not deliberate, much less policy. And – this is crucial – quality news organizations issue corrections and apologies. If coverage of Trump were a "left-wing conspiracy" as alleged, why would the *Journal* be among the publications most energetically revealing his misdeeds? The *Journal* is owned by Rupert Murdoch, who also owns Fox News.

CNN and MSNBC have unearthed major scoops about Trump; other news outlets have initiated outstanding spadework into his business and political dealings, including *The Hill* newspaper; magazines *The New Yorker*, *New York*, *The Atlantic* (edited by conservative David Frum), *Vanity Fair* and *Mother Jones;* along with websites such as ProPublica, The Daily Beast, Politico, Wired, BuzzFeed, ThinkProgress and HuffPost.

MEDIA STOOGES

The Toronto Star and British newspaper *The Guardian* regularly produce hard-hitting journalism about Trump.

Anyone who thinks that Trump and Nixon were singled out by the media needs to brush up on history. Every president over the past half century has endured uncomfortable scrutiny. The failed Bay of Pigs invasion in Cuba on John F. Kennedy's watch merited unflinching tough questioning. Lyndon Johnson declined to seek a second full term because public support for the Vietnam War had dwindled due in large part to assertive media attention. Reporters looked into whether Gerald Ford's pardon of Nixon resulted from an unsavory deal. Jimmy Carter faced critical reporting over the seizure of the U.S. Embassy in Tehran and botched attempt to rescue the hostages. Ronald Reagan and George H.W. Bush were rocked by revelations of the arms-for-hostages Iran-Contra scandal. Anyone who thinks Bill Clinton had it easy with the press should reread accounts of his time in office: Whitewater, the failed health care law, firing of the White House travel office, and numerous instances of womanizing all got unsparing treatment. George W. Bush was displeased with investigation into the Iraq invasion and its consequences. While Obama was president, the press looked vigorously into the Benghazi attack, Hillary Clinton's emails, health care legislation, accusations of IRS partisanship and numerous other events. Fairly or unfairly, all presidents experience exhaustive negative coverage.

Franklin Delano Roosevelt and Harry Truman, considered by historians to be among our greatest presidents, endured plenty of flak, but you have to wonder whether either could have politically survived the onslaught of hit jobs if Fox had existed in their day.

Potential candidates testing the waters for the 2020 presidential race are already seeing the press pile on. Do their résumés contain inconsistencies? Have they been associated with any unsavory characters? Who is donating to their campaign? How have they performed in public office they have already held? How do they treat their staff? What kind of investments or conflicts of interest do they have? Anyone who falls short will get unrelenting coverage by reporters poking around for the truth.

On the other side of the truth-o-meter, Fox News makes an effort to deliver a "message of the day" in as many news reports as possible. For example: when an undocumented alien, especially Hispanic, commits a serious crime or when a Central American gang member is apprehended at the U.S.-Mexico border, it is Fox's top story of the day. Why? Because it feeds Trump's narrative that Hispanics are menacing. It does not matter that aliens have a demonstrably lower crime rate than native-born Americans. Trump based the bedrock message of his candidacy on xenophobic hysteria. When the immigrant "caravan" slowly trudged northward through Mexico from Central America, bound for the U.S. border, Fox hyped breathlessly that they were criminals and terrorists planning to "invade" the United States. Other networks interviewed people along the route, who were fleeing violence and poverty, for human-interest stories. Many people who live hundreds of miles from the border voted for Trump for this anti-foreigner stance. They are afraid of Hispanics, and Trump delivered them a false solution by threatening to close the border and build a wall.

Fact: Roughly one hundred thousand Canadians live illegally in the United States, but Trump and Fox never mention this in their anti-immigrant frenzy. That's a lot of people. Don't you wonder why? Could it be because the Canadians are middle class and mostly white?

When the first case of Ebola appeared in the United States in 2014, Fox and its viewers went into panic mode. They shrieked that because Obama was "reckless" and "politically correct" (by not blocking travelers from Africa), the United States was on the verge of a pandemic. This caused widespread anxiety. Various government agencies worked with the Centers for Disease Control and contained the number of cases to under a dozen. If Ebola had originated in Europe instead of Africa, it's easy to think that the reaction would have been far different.

When researching *The Obama Haters*, I watched Fox News daily in 2009 and early 2010. The experience was akin to diving into a sewer. Each day I saw the since-disgraced Bill O'Reilly bloviate, along with Hannity and Glenn Beck, who since then left the network involuntarily.

After watching their reports, I checked facts for myself and every day I found numerous inaccuracies that would have been easy to spot before they went on the air. I remembered my experiences, and mistakes, in journalism school years ago and as a fledgling reporter. I concluded that the Fox windbags and their staffs either lacked the basic skills to find out the truth of what they were reporting, the skills any cub reporter should know, or they were intentionally ignoring or bending the facts. And it wasn't just me. Websites which check out facts, such as Snopes, FactCheck.org, and PolitiFact.com, reach the same conclusions on a regular basis. Fox News distorts its reporting, making a joke out of its "fair and balanced" slogan. When I monitored Fox, I was amazed that viewers could believe it since so many of the memes they repeat are easily debunked.

Fox brags that it tops its cable competitors on some prime time shows. During the Obama administration, Fox generally pulled in more than 1.5 million viewers during prime time, blowing out CNN and MSNBC combined. Does that mean they won the ratings war? Wait a sec. The traditional networks – CBS, NBC and ABC – claim seven million to eight million viewers apiece for their evening news broadcasts. Let that one sink in for a minute. Fox is simply a pretentious wannabe.

It's not that complicated to figure out. Many conservatives avoid mainstream newspapers because they are "biased" so they get nearly all their information from Fox, right-wing radio and right-wing websites. That totals about 1.5 million viewers. Liberals, moderates and independents are more willing to read newspapers and learn both sides of an issue. Combining the three networks, that's more than twenty million people. Add in CNN and MSNBC and you get another million. So now compare twenty-one million or twenty-two million people to 1.5 million at Fox. That's a lot of people getting a distorted view of the world, but they are a fraction of the entire population. You know someone is quoting Fox News when he or she says something like "the American people want to know" because that mimics the way Hannity and his posse phrase their statements to give the misconception that they represent the entire country.

Hosts on Fox echo Trump's deceptions with impunity. When Trump accused Hillary Clinton of "acid washing" her emails after receiving a subpoena in 2015, Hannity repeatedly made the claim throughout 2017 and 2018 even after it had been thoroughly disproved. Trump said in a 2016 tweet "why did she (Hillary) hammer 13 devices and acid-wash emails?" Even after the election, Trump continued to make the false claim, and Hannity was happy to repeat it *ad nauseam*. The FBI found that a contractor for a company which maintained Clinton's private server deleted the email archive with common software designed for that purpose. Fox News management does not seem to care that Hannity repeats falsehoods as long as he caters to its avid base and keeps ratings high. By mid-2018, Hannity began to spend most of his time attacking Mueller as he indicted one Trump associate after the next. But Fox doesn't fool everybody.

"The vehemence and irresponsibility of the rhetoric attacking the Mueller investigation tear at the very structure of our governance. Men who have sworn to use and protect our institutions of justice are steadily weakening them," Republican former Deputy Attorney General William Ruckelshaus wrote in August 2018 in *The Washington Post*. Ruckelshaus was fired by Nixon during the "Saturday Night Massacre" in October 1973 for refusing to dismiss Special Prosecutor Archibald Cox.

"Nixon was brought down by his disrespect for the law," Ruckelshaus continued. "It's hard to believe that forty-five years later, we may be in store for another damaging attack on the foundations of our democracy. Yet the cynical conduct of this president, his lawyers and a handful of congressional Republicans is frightening to me and should be to every citizen of this country." He concluded, "We need leaders who tell the truth. This is not now happening."

NEW TARGETS

After Trump took office, Fox hosts spent more time finding fault with Obama and Hillary, already out of power, than questions about Trump. After Democrats took back the House, Fox launched frequent salvos at Pelosi and Schumer, both objects of derision on the right. They've also found new targets: Massachusetts Senator Elizabeth Warren and New York Congresswoman Alexandria Ocasio-Cortez, who became well known so quickly that reporters now refer to her by her initials, AOC. There will be others. The right wing thrives on targets because it needs to divert attention from its own unpopular positions and leaders.

Warren said on numerous occasions that her family history counts Native Americans among her ancestors. Trump mocked her with the racist sobriquet Pocahontas. Florida Congressman Matt Gaetz followed that up with the equally racist Sacagawea. Instead of dismissing the ignorant remarks, Warren revealed DNA tests that backed her claim.

Ocasio-Cortez, whose heritage is Puerto Rican, is a newcomer, but so far she is doing a good job jabbing back at her detractors. Ocasio-Cortez is one of 435 members of the House and has no seniority, but the attacks began long before she won the election. Fox pounced on her because, although born in the Bronx, she lived some of her younger years in a middle-class suburb in Westchester County. Critics claimed that her biography as a girl from the Bronx was phony, somehow making her a less valid advocate for struggling people. Fox also bashed her wardrobe, accusing her of wearing high-end fashion (did they ever condemn Melania or Ivanka Trump for being fashionable?), although the clothing was just a loan for a photo shoot to accompany a magazine interview. Then, the morning chat show *Fox & Friends* ridiculed her for being unable to afford to rent an apartment in Washington D.C., prior to receiving her first congressional paycheck at a salary of $174,000 per year. Her withering riposte was that the show's hosts were obviously out of touch with Americans who struggle to pay rent. Why didn't the Foxies blast Texas Senator Ted Cruz's wife Heidi for grousing that her family can't afford to live on a congressional salary that is triple the median household income? Finally, the right wing got downright snarky when a YouTube video showed the now-congresswoman, while a student at Boston University, dancing along with other students in 2010 to recreate a scene from *The Breakfast Club*. On Twitter, she was called "America's favorite commie-know-it-all" and a "clueless nitwit." Dancing makes her a commie and a nitwit? What's wrong about having harmless fun with some fancy dance moves?

But it got even lower than this when GOP members booed a smiling Ocasio-Cortez while she voted for Pelosi as Speaker in her first act as a member of Congress. These are members of Congress paid to represent you and me, not TV commentators or bloggers. They denigrated a person most had never met and knew little about instead of jeering fellow Republicans who have made hateful or downright dangerous statements. Before casting aspersions on Ocasio-Cortez, righties need to look in their own crowded backyard, where there is plenty to condemn in their rogue's gallery of elected and appointed Republicans:

• Iowa Congressman Steve King, who displays a Confederate flag in his office, asserted that Mexicans crossing the border have "calves the size of cantaloupes because they're hauling seventy-five pounds of marijuana across the desert." In early 2019 he was at it again: "White nationalist, white supremacist, Western civilization – how did that language become offensive?" Despite a long record of spewing odious vocabulary, Trump proudly campaigned arm-in-arm with King.
• Texas Congressman Louie Gohmert accused Obama of being in league with radical Islamists: "This administration has so many Muslim Brotherhood members that have influence."
• South Carolina Congressman Joe Wilson heckled Obama's address to Congress in September 2009, shouting "You lie!" Wilson shamelessly used his outburst as a fund-raising tool even though fact checkers confirmed that Obama's speech was truthful. Such contemptible behavior should have benched Wilson, but instead Republicans promoted him to the leadership team in the House.

• Former Minnesota Congresswoman Michele Bachmann asserted that Obama was plotting to throw his political rivals in "FEMA" concentration camps. She also said that vaccinating adolescent girls against HPV (human papillomavirus) causes mental retardation. The American Academy of Pediatrics shot back: "There is absolutely no scientific validity to this statement."

• Former Alaska Governor Sarah Palin said so many nitwitty things that they could fill a library. Among her most outrageous was the fib that Obama's Affordable Care Act (Obamacare) would require sick people to plead for their lives before "death panels."

• North Carolina Congresswoman Virginia Foxx claimed that Obamacare is a greater threat than is terrorism.

• Former Missouri Congressman Todd Akin, as a Senate candidate, said a woman's body can prevent pregnancy in cases of "legitimate rape."

• Former Indiana Treasurer Richard Mourdock, as a Senate candidate, said when a woman is impregnated by a rapist "it's something God intended."

• Sharron Angle, challenging Harry Reid for his Nevada Senate seat in 2010, suggested the use of "Second Amendment remedies" if right wingers don't get their way. The Second Amendment of the Constitution pertains to gun rights.

• Sebastian Gorka, a former official in the Trump White House, told Hannity that Hillary Clinton should be executed for treason.

And all of this doesn't even include the countless baseless accusations that Obama was born in Kenya, a Muslim, a Communist, and on and on.

COLLUSION WITH RUSSIA IS "LEGAL"

Hannity and other Foxies often said that Hillary Clinton's private email account made her a criminal because the material could be stolen by a hostile agent and harm national security, even though the FBI concluded that this never happened. Hannity failed to mention that members of the Bush and Trump administration routinely did government business on personal email accounts and that Trump himself blurted out confidential information to Russian officials on numerous occasions. Yet Hannity said it would not be illegal if Trump or someone on his team intentionally worked together with Russia to manipulate the election, which the Mueller team is probing. Former federal prosecutors have said that any such activity would violate more than a dozen statutes. Collusion is another word for conspiracy, and conspiracy to commit a crime is always a crime, whether or not the crime is carried out. But Hannity sees it differently. Using Kafkaesque logic, he alleged that Mueller's "witch hunt" is a "soft coup" and is the real conspiracy against democracy. Hannity also accused former FBI Director James Comey of being a "hateful, vengeful, arrogant narcissist" who plotted to destroy Trump. He insisted Comey "abused power and fostered one of the most corrupt federal departments this country has ever seen." Hannity speculates that a "deep state" cabal within the U.S. government is working to bring down Trump, the exact words used by Putin. That raises the question about whether Hannity knows or cares that he is parroting Russian propaganda.

Fox's Tucker Carlson morphed himself into Hannity's conjoined twin by saying in late January 2019: "Mueller himself is a threat to our democracy, the most powerful man elected by nobody."

Anyone who hears such claptrap needs to think it through for a minute. Why would so many high-level people close to Trump confess to felonies or work out plea bargains if this was a set-up? If you are poor with a public defender, you might feel forced into a plea deal because the odds are stacked against you. But Trump's cronies have top-notch attorneys. If Mueller and Comey were bringing false charges, a world-class attorney representing high-profile people would fight it out in front of a jury. But they haven't. Trumpsters with the best lawyers have entered guilty pleas. Hannity is highly irresponsible to make such unfounded accusations. Prosecutorial misconduct is a serious crime, and there is no reason Mueller and his team would risk their case imploding if they lacked unimpeachable proof of wrongdoing.

Hannity and his clique are weakening America by dishonoring Mueller and other investigators. When people devoted to law enforcement or national security are disparaged and treated as scoundrels, it will be much harder to attract and retain qualified first-rate professionals.

Can you imagine a commentator in the 1970s accusing the Watergate investigators of being dirty? Hannity is accusing the FBI – the same people who arrested Bernie Madoff, Timothy McVeigh, John Gotti, the Unabomber, the Beltway Snipers, and the Enron crooks – of being criminals. Who benefits from

47

impugning the integrity of dedicated federal law-enforcement professionals, except Hannity's ratings? And why would advertisers want to participate in this unethical mendacity?

People who rise to the occasion and do the right thing at watershed moments are given high marks by history, while dead-enders who cling to the wrong side undergo permanent self-inflicted blemishes. Using Watergate as a reference point, history honors the men who stood up for the law: Sam Ervin chaired the Senate hearings, Elliott Richardson quit as attorney general rather than dismiss special prosecutor Archibald Cox, Leon Jaworski took over as special prosecutor after Cox was fired, and White House counsel John Dean warned Nixon there was a "cancer on the presidency." On the other side, the long list of people who aided Nixon are judged harshly by history.

As much as Trump and his supporters try to discredit the investigators, it's likely that Mueller and his team will be seen as champions while the people they have indicted have already suffered loss of face, perhaps permanently.

Hannity ain't the only liar at the Fox feeding trough. *Fox & Friends* said crimes by Paul Manafort, Trump's campaign chairman, were committed "many years before he joined Trump." False. While his crimes go back to 2006, some of them were committed in 2016 and 2017. On another occasion, *Fox & Friends* said Comey had leaked "top secret information" about Trump. False. Another Fox News special report said Middle Eastern immigrants were responsible for an increase in violent crime in Sweden; Trump used that report to tell audiences that a terror attack had just occurred in that peaceful Scandinavian land. Swedes were dumbfounded by the bigoted, ridiculous falsification. Fox asserted that the Obama administration released at least 122 prisoners from Guantanamo who "have returned to the battlefield." False. The Director of National Intelligence said Bush released 532 detainees, of whom 113 returned to the battlefield and that Obama freed 161, of whom nine rejoined Al-Qaeda.

Hannity and Trump tag teamed on numerous occasions with accusations that Democrats colluded with Russia. There is no reason to suspect this laughable narrative: Hillary Clinton was harmed, not helped, by Russian hacking. Trump griped that the twenty-five million dollars spent by the Mueller investigation is "millions of dollars of wasted money" even though thirty-four people were either indicted or pleaded guilty through early February 2019. By comparison, congressional Republicans frittered away thirty million dollars to investigate Hillary's Clinton's email and the Benghazi tragedy in Libya. Total indictments: Zero.

Day after day, so much evidence of Trump's acquiescence toward Russia races toward us that it's hard to keep track. But Fox either does not report this news, comes up with an excuse for Trump, or finds a way to blame it on Obama, the Clintons, Comey and Mueller.

There was a time Republicans and Fox respected law enforcement and national security agencies. That was prior to Trump. To be fair, some Fox hosts, such as Chris Wallace and Shepard Smith, have questioned Trump's fictions. But their skepticism occupies only a minuscule fraction of Fox's air time.

Too often Fox anchors give license to Trump and his cadre to spout off untruths, easily negated, without challenging them.

Except for Fox and other lapdogs, Trump is often belligerent toward the press. When CNN's Jim Acosta asked a tough question at a briefing, Trump revoked the correspondent's White House credentials. He called April Ryan, a reporter for American Urban Radio News, "nasty" and a "loser."

Trump is a frequent butt of jokes on comedy shows such as NBC's *Saturday Night Live*, the same as every president since the program began in 1975 with Chevy Chase lampooning Gerald Ford's pratfalls. Remember Tina Fey as Sarah Palin or Kate McKinnon's impersonations of Hillary Clinton? And who can forget Dana Carvey's spot-on portrayal of George H.W. Bush? But before Trump, no other president threatened retribution. "Nothing funny about tired Saturday Night Live on Fake News NBC! Question is, how do the Networks get away with these total Republican hit jobs without retribution? Likewise for many other shows? Very unfair and should be looked into. This is the real Collusion!" Trump tweeted February 17, 2019. "THE RIGGED AND CORRUPT MEDIA IS THE ENEMY OF THE PEOPLE!,"

In February 2016, Trump said he would "open up our libel laws so when they write purposely negative and horrible and false articles, we can sue them and win lots of money." In October 2017 he threatened to revoke the licenses of broadcasters he dislikes: "At what point is it appropriate to challenge their license?" Gordon Smith, a Republican former

Oregon senator and current president of the National Association of Broadcasters, countered: "The founders of our nation set as a cornerstone of our democracy the First Amendment, forever enshrining and protecting freedom of the press." If Trump was ever concerned about libel and facts, why did he join the racist "birther" brigade and accuse Obama of having a fake birth certificate?

Despite Trump's protestations about inaccuracy, nearly all of the negative off-the-record reports about his administration and the investigations are verified eventually by on-the-record sources, prosecutors, transcripts, and other documentation.

Both Clintons and Obama dealt with much more scurrilous coverage, most of it proved false and even loony. Obama was accused of being born in Kenya, being a Muslim, a Communist and terrorist sympathizer. One kook claimed to have had a gay sexual encounter with Obama. Bill Clinton was accused of corruption in Whitewater (a land deal in which he lost money), smuggling drugs through an air strip in Arkansas, and ordering the murder of a White House aide. Despite these ludicrous accusations by Fox and others, neither president ever tried to silence the press or take legal action against the smearmeisters.

Instead, they make ringing endorsements for independent law enforcement and a free press. Obama said in a September 7, 2018 speech at the University of Illinois: "It should not be a partisan issue to say that we do not pressure the attorney general or the FBI to use the criminal justice system as a cudgel to punish our political opponents. Or to explicitly call on the attorney general to protect members of our own party from prosecution because an election happens to be coming up. I'm not making that up. That's not hypothetical. It shouldn't be Democratic or Republican to say that we don't threaten the freedom of the press because they say things or publish stories we don't like. I complained plenty about Fox News, but you never heard me threaten to shut them down or call them enemies of the people. It shouldn't be Democratic or Republican to say we don't target certain groups of people based on what they look like or how they pray. We are Americans. We're supposed to stand up to bullies. Not follow them. We're supposed to stand up to discrimination, and we're sure as heck supposed to stand up clearly and unequivocally to Nazi sympathizers."

5

WITCH HUNT

How Trump Smears Investigations

A lie can travel half way around the world
while the truth is putting on its shoes

–Mark Twain (Samuel Clemens)

ARK TWAIN'S APHORISM, also attributed to Winston Churchill, suggests that lies spread more quickly than the truth, and some endure even after proved false. How many people still believe that Barack Obama is a Muslim, a Communist, foreign born, or any number of other untruths? Despite releasing his birth certificate authenticated by Hawaii state officials, the falsehoods persisted. Even though there was not a shred of evidence to sustain any of the absurd notions, millions of people continue to believe that Obama "does not love America." And it wasn't only Obama. Bill Clinton was accused of corruption in Whitewater (a land deal in which he lost money), smuggling drugs through an air strip in Arkansas, and ordering the murder of a White House aide. The only evidence of any wrongdoing on his part was a consensual affair with Monica Lewinsky, and that almost cost him his presidency. Twain certainly would get a big chuckle at our expense today.

Democrats controlled both Houses of Congress for only the first two out of Obama's eight years in the White House. During the remaining six years, Republicans used their authority to launch one fruitless investigation after the other into unsubstantiated allegations of misconduct by Obama and members of his administration. After spending millions of dollars and wasting the time of countless people, the results were clear by the end of Obama's presidency: No indictments. No arrests. No jail time for anyone connected to Obama. In other words, the cleanest administration in half a century. (Curiously, Congress continued to investigate Hillary Clinton's email "scandal" for the first two years of the Trump administration, with no results, until the Democrats took back control of the House of Representatives).

Some conservatives are ready to petition God and the Pope for Ronald Reagan's canonization. Yet, many Reagan acolytes might be surprised to be reminded that his years were marked by numerous scandals, leading to twenty-six indictments and sixteen convictions. That had been the largest number outside of Richard Nixon's White House, which saw seventy-six indictments and fifty-five convictions. During George W. Bush's two terms, sixteen indictments resulted in sixteen convictions.

Donald Trump seems to be competing with Nixon for the record, surpassing Reagan by early 2019. Special Prosecutor Robert Mueller indicted thirty-four people connected to Trump, among them prominent people in his inner circle. Michael

Cohen, Trump's personal attorney, pleaded guilty to violating campaign laws, among other crimes. Paul Manafort, his former campaign chair, faces years behind bars after conviction on eight charges of tax and bank fraud and is under further investigation for allegedly sharing campaign data with Russian agents. Michael Flynn, who shouted "Lock Her Up" about Hillary Clinton (she has never been charged with any crime) during 2016 campaign events and later Trump's national security adviser against Obama's advice, pleaded guilty to making false statements to the FBI. He is known to have shared confidential information with Russians. Senior campaign official Rick Gates confessed to tax and bank fraud. George Papadopoulos, a foreign policy adviser to the campaign, pleaded guilty to lying about contacts with Russians. Veteran right-wing hatchet man and Trump confidante Roger Stone, prominent for his WikiLeaks contacts, was indicted for obstruction of justice, witness tampering and lying to investigators. Also indicted were a Russian businessman for witness tampering, and Russian intelligence officers for hacking and leaking stolen Democratic campaign documents that damaged Clinton and helped Trump's candidacy. Trump has described some of those indicted and convicted as "good people" while dismissing the entire investigation as a "witch hunt."

These people who have been indicted and convicted, some of whom have confessed, are not peripheral characters with no direct access to Trump. Rather, they are central figures in his campaign and presidency, enough to make all of us nervous about the character and competence of the people holding pivotal positions in our government.

Merriam-Webster's Dictionary defines "witch hunt" as: "The searching out and deliberate harassment of those (such as political opponents) with unpopular views." Trump had repeated the term "witch hunt" 187 times by the end of 2018.

Trump amplified his own frenzied remarks in a February 7, 2019 tirade on Twitter as various congressional committees began hearings into his campaign, administration, and business dealings: "PRESIDENTIAL HARASSMENT! It should never be allowed to happen again!" and "The Republicans never did this to President Obama, there would be no time left to run government. I hear other committee heads will do the same thing. Even stealing people who work at White House! A continuation of Witch Hunt!"

Trump ignores the fact that Republicans investigated Obama's administration nonstop: Hillary Clinton's email, the Benghazi terrorist attack, federal loan guarantees to solar company Solyndra which went bankrupt, the canard that conservatives were harassed by the Internal Revenue Service, the "fast & furious" program that tracked gunrunning to Mexican criminals, the sale of Uranium One to a Russian company, assertions that Hillary Clinton would have been indicted over her email if not for her husband conspiring with then-Attorney General Loretta Lynch, and accusations that foreign donors to The Clinton Foundation got favors from Hillary Clinton as Secretary of State. Millions of taxpayer dollars were squandered chasing these imaginary rabbits down holes for eight years. No illegality was ever found. Yet in only two years, numerous indictments kept piling up on Trump allies.

A CNN poll in December 2018 found 59 percent of Americans believe Mueller's work is "a serious matter that should be fully investigated" while 35 percent think it is "mainly an effort to discredit Donald Trump's presidency." Fifty percent said Mueller's work "will implicate Donald Trump personally in wrongdoing" while 43 percent said such an outcome is unlikely. The same survey gave Trump a 39 percent approval rating and 55 percent disapproval. A *Washington Post* poll in February 2019 showed 61 percent of respondents would approve impeaching Trump if Mueller proves that the president authorized his campaign "to coordinate with the Russian government," but 33 percent oppose impeachment for those reasons.

ROBERT MUELLER

Trump has attacked Robert Mueller relentlessly on Twitter and elsewhere: "The inner workings of the Mueller investigation are a total mess," he tweeted in November 2018. "They have found no collusion and have gone absolutely nuts." He added, without providing evidence, that Mueller's team was "screaming and shouting at people, horribly threatening them to come up with the answers they want," and called the investigators "thugs," "a disgrace to our nation," and "highly conflicted."

This has emboldened apologists like Fox's Sean Hannity to mimic Trump's vicious condemnations and assassinate the character of devoted public servants.

Mueller, a Republican, heads the probe into allegations of wrongdoing in the Trump campaign and administration. The Vietnam veteran led the FBI for twelve years and served as a U.S. attorney and other top law-enforcement positions appointed by both presidents of both parties.

JAMES COMEY

Trump has disparaged James Comey, whom he fired as FBI director, labeling him, among other things, "not smart," "slippery" and a "slimeball." After Comey testified before Congress in December 2018, Trump said: "Leakin' James Comey must have set a record for who lied the most to Congress in one day. His Friday testimony was so untruthful!" Trump also called the Russia investigation a "Rigged Fraud."

Fact checkers have rebutted every Trump accusation against Comey.

Comey, a Republican, served for four years as FBI chief, a job for which he was confirmed 93-1 by the Senate. Trump ousted him in May 2017 under accusation of "not doing a good job." Earlier, he was named by President George W. Bush as a U.S. attorney and deputy attorney general.

ROB ROSENSTEIN

Trump accused Rob Rosenstein, the deputy attorney general who appointed Mueller, of treason. He released a tweet showing Rosenstein amid the faces of prominent Trump critics looking as if they were behind bars, with the words: "Now that Russia collusion is a proven lie, when do the trials for treason begin?" The other faces include Obama; Bill and Hillary Clinton; Mueller; Comey; John Podesta, chair of Hillary's presidential campaign; Houma Abedin, a former aide to Hillary; attorneys general during the Obama administration Eric Holder and Loretta Lynch; and James Clapper, Obama's head of National Intelligence.

An obvious question to such vilification is: What treasonous acts have these people committed? A second observation is that Russian collusion is not a "proven lie." The Mueller crew has already obtained numerous guilty pleas and convictions as it explores alleged links between people in Trump's orbit and Russia's plot to sabotage our elections and democracy.

Rosenstein, a Republican, was appointed by Trump as deputy attorney general in February 2017. Prior to that, he had served as a U.S. attorney under appointment by both Dubya and Obama.

Trump in May 2018 tweeted: "Why didn't the 13 Angry Democrats investigate the campaign of Crooked Hillary Clinton, many crimes, much Collusion with Russia? ... Why didn't the FBI take the Server from the DNC? Rigged

Investigation!" Trump has never identified the alleged "13 Angry Democrats," but they are believed to be some of the lawyers working for Mueller who Trump accuses of having "conflicts of interest." Mueller stresses that he never asked any of his investigators about their political allegiances.

No president since Nixon has condemned the investigations against them, even when some of their appointees went to jail. In fact, Reagan and both Bushes ate humble pie when faced with evidence of illegality involving their appointees. The difference was that even if they or someone in their orbit did something wrong, they believed in the rule of law. They worked to exorcise the cancerous growths on their presidencies and by doing so gained some redemption with the public, and with historians.

Trump, on the other hand, has never admitted wrongdoing. He praises associates accused of grotesque offenses against democracy while condemning those who have admitted their roles in skulduggery. This yet another throwback to Tricky Dick, and we all know where he ended up. For all his faults, Nixon at least was abundantly prepared for the office and had numerous real accomplishments which, unfortunately, are overshadowed by his heinous misdeeds. Among people old enough to remember Nixon, few hold him in esteem. Historical documents show him to have been dishonest. Would we want a parent or grandparent to tell us that the president whose name is synonymous with Watergate and presidential misconduct was railroaded? Similarly, future generations will want to know what we did to protect our nation from Trump.

60

WITCH HUNT

Trump's fatuous "witch hunt" argument against Mueller was effectively laid to rest January 15, 2019 when Robert Barr, in his Senate confirmation hearings for attorney general, said, "I don't believe Mr. Mueller would be involved in a witch hunt." Since that is the sworn testimony of the nation's top law-enforcement officer, Barr knocked the wind out of the shopworn "witch hunt" fabrication.

OTHER INVESTIGATIONS

Mueller's probe into Russian connections is only one among numerous investigations swirling around Trump. Mueller is reportedly digging into ties the Trump campaign may have had with the United Arab Emirates, Saudi Arabia and Israel and how those foreign actors might have influenced the election.

And it's not just Mueller. Federal prosecutors in New York are examining Trump's business dealings, tipped off by Cohen's confessions. Prosecutors issued subpoenas to Trump's inaugural committee on suspicion that Russian and other foreign hotshots who attended the festivities may have made illegal donations for access to the new president. They are also looking into secretive contributions to a SuperPAC (political action committee) which helped Trump and his allies who lobbied for Ukraine. Prosecutors are attempting to obtain further information from Marina Butina about a possible relationship with the Trump campaign. She was convicted of conspiracy to act as an illegal foreign agent for Russia after worming her way into the National Rifle Association (NRA) and other conservative organizations. Prosecutors in Maryland and Washington D.C. have subpoenaed documents to determine whether Trump, through his business holdings, has violated the emoluments clause in the Constitution which prohibits receiving money from foreign governments

There's enough suspicious behavior to occupy investigators and prosecutors for quite some time. New York's new attorney general, Letitia James, is launching extensive probes of the Trump family and inner circle involving real estate deals, Trump Tower meetings with Russian agents, the now-defunct Trump Foundation, and other purported crimes committed in the Empire state. James could be a key figure for her unique position. The president has the authority to pardon anyone convicted of a federal crime, giving him leverage over cronies who are sentenced but hide his possible involvement. The pardon power, however, can only go so far: a president can only absolve people convicted of federal crimes, not state crimes.

6

ENVIRONMENTAL DISGRACE

What World Are We Leaving Our Grandchildren?

And I brought you into a plentiful country, to eat the fruit
thereof and the goodness thereof; but when ye entered, ye
defiled my land, and made mine heritage an abomination

–Jeremiah 2:7

N O SANE PERSON would knowingly harm his or her children or grandchildren. Then why would otherwise rational people vote for political leaders who pursue policies which threaten the viability of the world we occupy, which we hope will be inhabited by our descendants after our own time has passed? Our use of energy is a benefit that carries responsibility. Sure, we all want to drive our cars, take airplanes to vacation in Hawaii or Europe, heat our homes in the winter and cool them in the summer. We don't want to live in the caves of our ancient ancestors; we enjoy the comforts of modern life. But do those conveniences endanger, or even doom, our heirs? This question is posed by people who spend their lives studying the environment.

Once again we need to look at our behavior from the prism of history. Many historians today believe Donald Trump will be judged unfavorably by historians of the future for his rash behavior and destruction of the norms by which his predecessors treated the office. Likewise, future historians will judge us. We can't see into the future, but climate scientists almost universally believe that human activity causes global warming which leads to weather anomalies that kill people and destroy communities. Most Americans agree.

A Gallup poll conducted in 2018 showed 60 percent of the population believe Trump does a poor job protecting the environment, versus 31 percent who think he is doing a good job. By comparison, 54 percent in 2016 thought Barack Obama did a credible job on the environment, while 39 percent said he did not. Most Americans want the government to actively preserve the environment. The Gallup survey showed just 9 percent believe the government is doing too much to protect the environment (so much for the "government overreach" fallacy), while 62 percent say it does too little, and 28 percent agree that it is doing the right amount. Clear majorities oppose expanding nuclear energy use, opening federal lands for more oil exploration, subsidies for the coal industry, and allowing oil exploration in the Arctic National Wildlife Refuge. Substantial majorities favor stronger enforcement of environmental regulations, tougher emissions standards, increased investments in renewable energy sources, mandatory controls on greenhouse gases, stricter rules on fracking, and a carbon tax.

So won't we be judged as a society for allowing Trump to gut pollution regulations, abandon the landmark Paris climate agreement and hand over national monuments to energy companies which donate generously to political campaigns? A *Washington Post*-ABC poll in 2017 revealed that 59 percent of Americans opposed dumping the Paris accords, as opposed to 28 percent who agreed with Trump's withdrawal.

Trump showed his contempt for the environment by appointing unqualified people with egregious conflicts of interest to serve as custodians of our irreplaceable natural resources.

Trump tapped Oklahoma Attorney General Scott Pruitt to run the Environmental Protection Agency, known as EPA. Pruitt showed such hostility to the agency that before running the EPA, he sued it thirteen times to reverse pollution rules. He even challenged EPA's mission, saying it "was never intended to be our nation's foremost environmental regulator."

Conservative Richard Nixon might argue otherwise, since he established EPA in 1970 to protect the environment by consolidating various departments under one umbrella. He appointed William Ruckelshaus, a true believer in the cause, as its first chief. The agency monitors compliance with environmental regulations and administers the "superfund" to clean up degraded areas. It regulates fuel economy and vehicle emissions while overseeing oil spill cleanup, toxic releases, underground storage tanks, clean drinking water, radioactive waste, mercury emissions and mining wastewater. In recent years, it has also worked toward implementing regulations to combat climate change.

Pruitt was dogged by a dizzying array of ethical lapses during his abbreviated tenure. The most secretive EPA chief in

65

history, Pruitt concealed information about his meetings, speaking events and trips. He got below-market rent on an apartment in Washington D.C. thanks to an industry lobbyist. Unlike his predecessors, Pruitt flew first class on commercial flights as well as chartering private jets or military planes whenever he could. He billed the taxpayers for luxury hotels. During a trip to Morocco, which cost seventeen thousand dollars, he promoted exports of liquefied natural gas (LNG), and then took a two-day layover in Paris on the public dime. To isolate himself from outside eyes and ears, Pruitt ordered construction of a forty-three-thousand-dollar soundproof booth at his office. He forced subordinates to book his hotel rooms on their personal credit cards and did not reimburse them, and he made them work to help his wife obtain a franchise with fast-food company Chick-fil-A.

Pruitt's depredations of the environment were even worse than his fleecing of taxpayers. He told CNBC that he doubted carbon dioxide was a primary contributor to global warming, countering EPA's own website. Trump slashed spending on the environment. His first budget ordered 24 percent cuts in EPA funding and a 20 percent staff reduction. Pruitt fired scientists from the agency's eighteen-member Board of Scientific Counselors to replace them with industry insiders. He met with industry lobbyists frequently but almost never with environmentalists. The Environmental Integrity Project disclosed that the Trump administration was collecting 60 percent less money in environmental fines. Pruitt removed, relaxed or delayed sixty-seven environmental regulations.

ENVIRONMENTAL DISGRACE

Pruitt headed for the exit when his ethical violations became an embarrassment for Trump, who nevertheless said publicly that he had "done an outstanding job." Trump replaced him with Andrew Wheeler, a former coal industry lobbyist who is also a climate change skeptic. Wheeler signaled his intention to go to bat for the coal industry by fighting regulations. Trump rolled back Obama-era rules prohibiting disposal of coal ash from power plants in public waterways, which poses a risk to drinking water for millions of Americans. He also gave the coal industry a generous gift by rolling back restrictions on greenhouse gas in coal-fired power plants, a move seen as encouraging the construction of new coal plants after shutdowns in recent years.

Pruitt wasn't the only hack who lavishly spent taxpayer money on his own questionable perks while exploiting his position to degrade the environment instead of protecting it. He was matched by Interior Secretary Ryan Zinke, head of the department responsible for managing federal lands, including national parks, wildlife refuges, minerals and Native American reserves. The position has been occupied by respected environmental champions such as Stuart Udall (appointed by John F. Kennedy), Cecil Andrus (Jimmy Carter), Bruce Babbitt (Bill Clinton), Ken Salazar (Obama), and Sally Jewell (Obama), CEO of outdoor supplies retailer Recreational Equipment Inc. (REI). Reagan was a notable exception, appointing notorious anti-environmental activist James Watt to the post, but Trump did him one better. Zinke's tenure, lasting less than two years, was marked by endless ethical investigations into his myriad conflicts of interest. He slashed federal ownership at Bears Ears and Grand Staircase-Escalante National Monuments, both in Utah. He also tried to shrink the size of Nevada's Gold Butte and Oregon's Cascade-Siskiyou National Monuments, as well as weaken oversight at six others. Internal documents obtained by *The New York Times* showed these moves were aimed to increase industry access to coal, oil and natural gas. But Zinke's downfall came after Republicans were embarrassed when he hitched rides on corporate jets from companies with business before the department and costly leases of private airplanes to make speeches. He remains under investigation for a fishy land deal in Montana and fourteen other topics. Zinke's replacement is David Bernhardt, a former lobbyist for the oil industry.

Zinke and Pruitt were not the only bad apples among Trump's environmental appointees. Onis "Trey" Glenn III quit as EPA's Region 4 administrator in November 2018 after being indicted for ethics violations in Alabama. Glenn was charged with allegedly helping the Drummond Company, whose CEO was convicted of bribery related to opposing a listing on EPA's priority cleanup list. This wasn't Glenn's first ethics rodeo. The Alabama Ethics Commission in 2007 found probable cause that he had violated state laws for accepting gifts from companies with business before the Alabama Department of Environmental Management, which he ran at the time.

Energy Secretary Rick Perry, the former governor of Texas, is a climate change skeptic. He shifted gears toward subsidizing coal and away from the Obama-era focus on renewable fuel initiatives. He described renewable energy as "immoral."

Trump claimed that minimizing Bears Ears and Grand Staircase-Escalante supported the will of Utah residents, even though 91 percent of Beehive State residents disagreed with his giveaway. Trump defended his decision, saying: "Some people think that the natural resources should be controlled by a small handful of very distant bureaucrats located in Washington ... And guess what: They're wrong."

The "distant bureaucrats" protecting federal lands are in reality the perfect example of democracy in action, with everyone getting a say. In Oregon, when the heavily armed renegade Bundy family and its henchmen overran the Malheur National Wildlife Refuge in early 2016, some touted them as right-wing champions against "big government" and "federal overreach." The late novelist Ursula Le Guin penned an essay in her hometown newspaper *The Oregonian* which put the concept of public lands in perspective: "I can't go to the Malheur refuge now, though as a citizen of the United States, I own it and have the freedom of it. That's what public land is: land that belongs to the public – me, you, every law-abiding American," she wrote. "Those citizens of Harney County have carefully hammered out agreements to manage the refuge in the best interest of landowners, scientists, visitors, tourists, livestock and wildlife."

As for distant bureaucrats allegedly making decisions about federal lands, those determinations will now be made instead by faraway corporate boards of directors with no input from the public. Hikers, fishermen, archeologists, plant and wildlife experts and everyone else without a seat on corporate boards will be shut out of the deliberations which will govern the fate of what used to be treasures for all to enjoy at national monuments.

Trump's odious environmental legacy is a checklist of servile bootlicking for energy companies and polluters at the expense of the environment:

• He gave a green light to the Keystone XL pipeline to carry 800,000 barrels per day of toxic, heavy crude oil from Canada to the U.S. Gulf Coast, mostly for export. Obama had rejected the permit application on environmental grounds based on a State Department study as well as complaints by private landowners in Nebraska and native tribal communities in the Dakotas.
• Trump issued an executive order instructing agencies to increase logging 31 percent on federal lands after blaming poor forest management for record wildfire damage in 2018.
• Criminal prosecutions at EPA are at the lowest rate in thirty years and at little over one-quarter the level of the Clinton years.
• The Interior Department eased restrictions on oil and gas drilling on millions of acres of protected habitat in eleven western states.
• The Trump administration approved offshore drilling in the Arctic Ocean north of Alaska from an artificial island and granted the largest-ever lease auction of oil and natural gas rights in the Gulf of Mexico. Obama had tightened leasing in Gulf waters after the tragic 2010 Deepwater Horizon disaster, the worst oil spill in U.S. history.
• EPA rescinded Obama's incremental fuel efficiency standards.
• Trump eliminated worldwide carbon monitoring by the National Aeronautics and Space Administration (NASA).
• EPA weakened protections for endangered species.

- Trump gutted investment in clean energy programs and climate change research.
- The administration scrapped Obama's clean power plan, designed to cut the sector's emissions by 32 percent through 2030, which Trump and his allies described as a "war on coal."
- Trump killed a study of health risks to residents who live near mountaintop removal coal mining sites in the Appalachian region.
- The president removed climate change from the list of national security threats. The Obama administration in 2015 called climate change "an urgent and growing threat to our national security" due to its effects on natural disasters, food and water conflicts and refugee crises.
- He later formed a group to study whether climate change is a national security threat; the panel included a climate change denier who argues that greenhouse gases are a benefit.
- Nine of the twelve members of the civilian National Parks System Advisory Board, formed in 1935, resigned to protest the Trump administration's refusal to consider their input.

Granted, the record is not exclusively negative. On a lonely positive note, Trump signed a law to improve cleanup of plastic trash from the world's oceans.

Trump's overall impact on the environment was best summarized by Michael Cox, who upon his retirement in March 2017 after working at the agency since 1987, wrote an open letter to Pruitt. Cox worked as a climate change adviser for the EPA's Seattle office.

"This is the first time I remember staff openly dismissing and mocking the environmental policies of an administration," Cox wrote. "The message we are hearing is that this administration is working to dismantle the EPA and its staff as quickly as possible." He decried Pruitt's denial of fundamental climate science. "It was surprising, no shocking, when you stated on national television that carbon dioxide is not a primary contributor to climate change. This is settled science and we have too many other important scientific issues to investigate related to climate change to waste our time debating this issue."

Cox questioned whether the energy industry was pulling the strings behind Trump's environmental actions. "We are frankly insulted that the president would come to EPA to announce that he is overturning the work to battle the most urgent environmental problem of our generation – climate change," Cox wrote. He accused Trump of giving "false hope" to coal miners who have lost their jobs. "The cause of the decline was simple: automation, not job killing regulations."

The letter said Pruitt was "appointing political staff who are openly hostile to EPA" and "continuing to demonize the EPA." He said Pruitt had a "lack of understanding of what we do at EPA." Cox ended with: "The health of the American people and our country depends on you."

7

WHAT DO WE TELL THE CHILDREN?

Compassion is the basis of morality

–Arthur Schopenhauer

IS DONALD TRUMP a compassionate man? From threatening to jail his political opponents and urging protesters be beaten to intentionally separating children of refugees and ridiculing people suffering from disabilities or tragedies, Trump has shown a disturbing lack of compassion for others. While Bill Clinton, despite all his faults, could "feel your pain," Trump dehumanizes others and compounds their suffering. Does this matter? Do we value compassion in our leaders? Should we?

Numerous psychiatrists and psychologists, although they have not personally counseled Trump, suggest he suffers from narcissistic personality disorder. We have all met the type: insecure, egocentric, vengeful, cowardly, petty, petulant, spiteful, braggart, a compulsive need for admiration, inability to accept criticism, and contempt for others. Most of us tend to avoid these people when we can, but when we are forced to deal with such behavior we learn coping mechanisms. One thing for certain is that we don't trust such people. We know they only look out for Number One, and we teach youngsters that this is wrong.

So, how do we react when our children ask us what they have heard about their president? Another question we should all consider is how we would react if our children, or any member of our family, comported themselves like Trump.

"RESPECT THE PRESIDENCY"

Someone told me that he was upset about Robert De Niro's foul-mouthed invective against Trump at the 2018 Tony Awards. "That's not the time and place for it. We should respect the office of the president," he groused.

Yes, De Niro's descriptions were crude and certainly not in keeping with traditional deference toward the president. But De Niro wasn't the first to lace into a president. Numerous entertainers, as well as public officials, had called Barack Obama un-American, a Communist, a terrorist, as well as every imaginable racist taunt. Rock musician Ted Nugent said in 2012 that if Obama was re-elected, he would "either be dead or in jail by this time next year."

In fact, Trump himself sullied the presidency by endorsing the "birther" conspiracy, racist hokum that Obama was born in Kenya rather than his native Honolulu. When asked about it, Trump claimed that Hillary Clinton started the smear. Not true. She had quipped about it once because it was so ludicrous. Obama himself simply lampooned those who spread it, including Trump himself at the White House Correspondents Dinner in 2011.

Obama, while critical of Bush's Iraq invasion and economic policies that brought about the worst economic crisis since the Great Depression, was never disrespectful toward his predecessor.

So, yes, we need to tell children to respect the president and the presidency. But if they hear terrible things about Trump, we must be honest and explain that his behavior does not represent the values of most Americans.

CANDIDACY ANNOUNCEMENT

Trump launched his campaign on a false premise, oozing racism and bigotry after riding down an escalator in Trump Tower. "When Mexico sends its people, they're not sending their best," he said. "They're sending people that have lots of problems, and they're bringing those problems to us. They're bringing drugs. They're bringing crime. They're rapists. And some, I assume, are good people."

Research shows otherwise. Data in many respected studies prove that immigrants have a lower crime rate than native-born Americans. Trump's remarks ginned up fears of undocumented immigrants in general and Mexicans in particular. As an American who lived in Mexico as a foreign correspondent, I can attest that Trump's remarks are blatantly wrong. Mexico does not officially send anyone, but Mexicans who emigrate northward, legally or illegally, are overwhelmingly ambitious, honest citizens. The vast majority come to work hard and save money to either send back to

75

family or to take home later to buy a house, start a business, or retire. True, criminals do bring drugs across the border, but few of them are the immigrants. Drugs are smuggled on boats, airplanes, underground tunnels, and concealed in vehicles which cross the border at legal checkpoints. Border security is inarguably vital, but more walls won't keep out drugs. Conflating Mexicans who cross the border to harvest crops, wash dishes, work as gardeners, or take care of our children and senior citizens, with drug smugglers and other criminals belies the facts and is racially slanted. Like any demagogue, Trump conjures up an outside menace to stoke fear and loathing.

Do we really believe that all Mexicans are rapists and criminals? Is that the message we as a society want to impart to our children and to Hispanic children? Fifty-two million Hispanics live in the United States. Will we endorse a message of hate originating from our president?

LIES

One of the stories we hear as youngsters is that George Washington, when confronted by his father, confessed to chopping down a cherry tree. Truth or folklore, the message is clear: we want to instill the importance of telling the truth, and children learn by example. Family, teachers, everyone is measured by that yardstick.

While no one may be truthful 100 percent of the time, we want our role models to be upstanding. So how do we respond to the revelation by *The Washington Post* that Trump was caught in 8,158 "false or misleading claims" during his first two years in office? The newspaper tabulated 8.9 lies per day in 2018, up from 2.9 daily fibs in 2017. The *Post's* "Fact Checker Database" through the end of 2018 lists Trump's most common false or misleading claims, then lays out the facts and tells how many times they were repeated. One whopper concerning the FBI investigation was repeated 187 times.

And it started on his first day in office when his press secretary insisted his inauguration had "the largest audience to ever witness an inauguration" even though comparative photos showed far more people attended when Obama took office. The truth was humiliating, so the White House doctored the crowd photos to make it look like more people were there. Experts estimated Trump's crowd at one hundred fifty thousand people, about one-quarter of the throng who had watched Obama's swearing-in eight years earlier. When caught in a falsehood, the Trump White House said it is using "alternative facts." A lie is still a lie.

Honest Abe called it right when he said, "No man has a good enough memory to be a successful liar."

True, not all presidents were moral paragons. After Richard Nixon's disgrace, the nation welcomed an Eagle Scout as president in Gerald Ford. And he was succeeded by another Boy Scout, Jimmy Carter. Neither was considered among our most effective presidents or top-tier leaders, but their character served as a role model for us all and history views their moral direction warmly.

Later came Obama, a committed family man who was never accused of any wrongdoing. His administration was the cleanest in the modern era. No top aide was forced out for ethical lapses. After eight years, no official in his administration went to jail. Yet viewers of Fox News are still told that his administration was riddled with corruption and that he hates America. Nobody explains how he was corrupt or why he allegedly does not love America, but vicious propaganda exerts power over ill-informed people.

Obama was followed by Trump, who in short order saw numerous close associates in his business life, campaign, and White House, indicted for many different crimes.

We all know politicians stretch the truth to their advantage, but Trump has made an art form out of mendacity. We need to learn from the past, elect another moral Boy or Girl Scout and recover the honor of the Oval Office.

CONSERVATIVE OPPOSITION

All presidents face vigorous pushback from the other side. No matter what they propose, their political opponents will try to knock it down or least force some compromises. That's the normal give and take. But many of Trump's fiercest critics are fellow Republicans, though woefully few are current office holders. Furthermore, he has drawn many people out of the shadows who don't usually get involved in partisan politics.

During the presidential campaign in September 2016, seventy-five retired career Foreign Service officers who served under Republican and Democratic presidents, signed an open letter calling Donald Trump "entirely unqualified to serve as president and commander in chief ... this is the first time many of us have publicly endorsed a candidate for president."

That followed a petition by more than a hundred Republican national security experts saying publicly that they would never work in a Trump administration and fifty other Republican former Cabinet secretaries and other aides saying Trump would be "the most reckless president in American history."

These were unprecedented moves by so many people of this caliber. Never before did such a mass movement focus on integrity irrespective of ideology.

And, they were right. Trump's foreign policy moves have been a disaster and run contrary to decades or centuries of American policies: angering or humiliating close allies like Canada, Mexico, the United Kingdom, France, and Germany, while playing footsie with Vladimir Putin, North Korea, Turkey and the Saudis. Trump weakened NATO by saying he would not defend our tiny Baltic allies or Macedonia, once part of the former Yugoslavia. Then he mused about quitting the North Atlantic alliance. Our allies fighting terrorism in Syria were dumbfounded when Trump, without warning, announced withdrawal from that hotspot, delighting guess who, Putin. Trump frequently sides against our own intelligence security services to ally with Putin. He insults political opponents on a daily basis.

Recent presidents were often described in positive terms by people holding opposing views who knew them personally. Ronald Reagan, both Bushes, Bill Clinton and Obama were liked on a personal level, even by political adversaries. Former members of their administrations remain devoted long after leaving office. Not so with Trump. Through the years, many people who did business with him have nothing positive to say. Not many people who departed after working for his campaign or administration hold him in esteem. Everyone in public life, from politicians and titans of industry to entertainers and athletes, has detractors. But when someone's one-time allies keep pointing to character flaws, you've got to wonder what's wrong.

Former Secretary of State Rex Tillerson was quoted calling him a "moron." Defense Secretary Jim Mattis' resignation letter lamented Trump's willingness to cozy up to Russia and let down allies. Then-Chief of Staff John Kelly called Trump an "idiot" and described the White House staff as operating in "crazytown." After former aide Omarosa Manigault-Newman said she had recordings of Trump using racial slurs, he called her a "dog." Mia Love, a Republican member of Congress from Utah who lost her seat in a paper-thin 2018 election, said Trump has "no real relationships, just convenient transactions." Even after Trump tried to curry favor with conservative columnist Ann Coulter, she returned the favor by saying, "The only national emergency is that our president is an idiot." Trump's former long-time personal lawyer, Michael Cohen, was equally strident, asserting that the president "directed" him to commit crimes, including lying to Congress, and described "what it's like to work for a madman." Andrew McCabe, who spent years taking down organized crime capos before Trump fired him as acting FBI director, described the president's personal loyalty demands as "classic criminal enterprise behavior."

Knowing all we know, it is keenly unsettling that so few elected Republicans are willing to call out Trump. John McCain used his gravitas and stature to do so. "We weaken our greatness when we confuse our patriotism with tribal rivalries that have sown resentment and hatred and violence in all the corners of the globe," McCain wrote a farewell letter to the world shortly before his death. "Do not despair of our present difficulties but believe always in the promise and greatness of America, because nothing is inevitable here. Americans never quit. We never surrender. We never hide from history. We make history."

The eulogies at McCain's funeral, by his former rivals George W. Bush and Obama, and the absence of Trump from the guest list, were a powerful reminder to the nation about measuring the life of a man who served with distinction and courage in sharp contrast to Trump. Four months later, the passing of George H.W. Bush brought the same spotlight on a man who served his country most of his ninety-four years, once again revealing Trump's glaring faults. The Bush family was not shy about saying they refused to vote for Trump. Poppy Bush voted for Hillary Clinton. Barbara Bush, before she died in April 2018, reinforced her reputation for brusqueness by saying: "I don't know how women can vote for Trump" and "I'm sick of him."

Senators Jeff Flake of Arizona and Bob Corker of Tennessee stood up to Trump numerous times, but both were lame ducks who declined to seek another term in 2018 and left office the following January.

It is also noteworthy to point out that after the deaths of McCain and Bush Senior, liberals and Democrats displayed genuine affection for both, notwithstanding political differences. Contrast that to the outright unrelenting hatefest orchestrated by Trump and the right wing toward the Clintons and Obama.

FROM RUSSIA WITHOUT LOVE

Following the end of the Second World War, conservative Republicans took a consistent no-quarter approach to dealing with the Soviet Union. They often labeled Democrats and liberals as "un-American" if they tried to even negotiate with the Soviets. After the Berlin Wall tumbled in 1989, President George H.W. Bush proclaimed a "new world order" in which Russia could move toward becoming a reliable ally and guarantee a more peaceful planet. Liberals and conservatives alike rejoiced, and leaders of both parties saw the "peace dividend" as allowing us to rein in the exorbitant military budget and redirect government revenues to other needs. Mikhail Gorbachev was succeeded by Boris Yeltsin, and we continued warm relations with Russia. Yeltsin was followed by Putin in a free and fair election, and it looked as though democracy and free markets had taken root in the world's original Communist state after seven decades. But it became obvious that Putin intended to stay in power longer than we thought, and he began to flex his power with brute force. Then the mask was ripped off by incursions into former Soviet satellites, the poisoning of Ukraine President Viktor Yuschenko, the assassinations of Russian turncoats in the West, and the June 2014 downing of a commercial airplane by pro-Russia forces in Ukraine.

Under Obama, the U.S. government and its European allies together imposed economic sanctions. During the 2016 presidential campaign, Hillary Clinton vowed to squeeze sanctions tighter on Putin, describing him as a "thug" while Trump called him "so nice," sending out an olive branch interpreted by some as a white flag. Little by little, U.S. intelligence became aware that WikiLeaks was working in tandem with Russia to hack documents from the Clinton campaign and expose them. The leaks, which never showed wrongdoing but embarrassed the Clinton team, always worked in Trump's favor. Trump himself encouraged the hacking. He said at a July 2016 press conference, "Russia, if you're listening, I hope you're able to find the thirty-thousand emails that are missing." And Putin even publicly admitted that he favored the real estate mogul.

Then came the famous Helsinki summit in July 2018, when Trump said he believed Putin more than U.S. intelligence agency assessments that pointed to Russian interference in our election. Republican Congressman Will Hurd of Texas, a former undercover CIA operative in Central Asia, said: "I've seen Russian intelligence manipulate many people over my professional career and I never thought that the US president would become one of the ones getting played by old KGB hands."

A few other Republicans disapproved, but most tried to change the subject as Trump handed Russia its greatest foreign policy coup since the end of the Cold War. Critics wondered aloud whether Putin had dirt on Trump which he used as leverage. They pointed to Trump's business history, asserting that he has made deals with Russians who have connections to the government and/or criminals, and that this would be exposed if he stood up to Moscow. Robert Mueller's investigation is studying those potential links, even looking into whether Trump himself might be a Russian agent. Russians have long had a word to describe someone who does their bidding, willingly or unwillingly: useful idiot. Sadly, much of the world, including our allies and adversaries, believes that Trump serves that role.

It wasn't only in Helsinki. Trump has a disturbing habit of parroting Russian propaganda. In one instance, his National Security Council alleged that Belarus was at risk of an invasion by Poland, an idea pushed by Putin as a pretext to boost his military presence in Belarus, ruled by a Moscow-allied dictator. Another time, Trump told Fox News that the people of Montenegro, a former Yugoslav republic with anti-Russian leanings, are so "aggressive" that they are capable of starting a Third World War. More blatant talking points by Russia, which plotted to overthrow the Montenegro government to keep it out of NATO. By early 2019, Trump was not only rationalizing Russian spin, but also pleading the case of the former Soviet Union. He upended a century of U.S. foreign policy of confronting Russian aggression by endorsing the Soviets' 1979 invasion of Afghanistan. "The reason Russia was in Afghanistan was because terrorists were going into Russia," Trump said. "They were right to be there." Would Ronald Reagan agree? National Security experts told *The New York Times* that Trump on several occasions discussed wanting to abandon NATO. That would destroy the Western alliance and hand Putin everything he wanted on a silver, no golden, platter. Trump, after a 2017 meeting with Putin in Hamburg, grabbed the written notes from his interpreter, the lone witness, and ordered him to secrecy. At another Trump-Putin session, the only other person attending was Russia's interpreter. We learn that such meetings took place only because the Russians report them, after which the White House grudgingly is forced to admit what it was hiding from the public. Russia experts and former diplomats vehemently described these incidents as unprecedented and horrifying.

Still, Trump's base did not abandon him despite the alarming reversal in what had been an unwavering U.S. foreign policy position. Fox News instructed viewers to ignore Trump's prostrations to Russia and instead grouse about a new Democratic member of Congress who used salty language to describe the president.

Fox's Tucker Carlson, rather than expressing shock over a possible pullout from NATO, instead questioned the need for the alliance, considered bedrock to the defense of the United States and Europe. "Vladimir Putin runs Russia now. He does not plan to invade Western Europe. He can't. So why do we still have NATO?" Carlson said on January 15, 2019. "In the 1990s, our leaders decided it would be a wise idea to promise countries like Latvia and Estonia that we'd use nuclear weapons to protect them if they ever had a problem with Russia. Why did we do that? Well, who knows? The details are lost to history."

Sorry Tucker, but not a single detail is lost. The Soviet Union existed for seven decades, during which Russia overran fourteen republics as part of its "union." After the Second World War, the Soviet Union occupied eight countries behind the "Iron Curtain" in Eastern Europe. Since the fall of the Berlin Wall and disintegration of the Soviet empire in 1991, Russia invaded Georgia and Ukraine and annexed Crimea. It has threatened other neighbors, and foreign policy experts of all political genres overwhelmingly endorse NATO as Europe's best protection from invasion. Period. The fact that Putin actively strives to hobble NATO is proof that we shouldn't let that happen. Does anyone truly believe that conservative patron saint Ronald Reagan would countenance any move to weaken NATO or embolden Russia? Like his predecessors, Obama supported America's longstanding military and economic alliances unflinchingly.

WHAT DO WE TELL THE CHILDREN?

In early 2019, Trump eased Obama's sanctions on Russian Oleg Deripaska, a Putin-allied oligarch with links to Trump's former campaign chairman Paul Manafort and accused of money laundering, extortion and murder-for-hire. Democrats sought to block the move, but only eleven Republicans joined them, short of the two-thirds vote necessary. More cheering in the Kremlin.

Trump and his follows have repeated "there was no collusion with the Russians" so many times it could be their mantra. As evidence piled up, Rudy Giuliani, the former New York mayor and a Trump lawyer, tacitly acknowledged in early 2019 that collusion occurred, despite having denied it hundreds of times, but this time he insisted that Trump was not personally involved. At least sixteen people associated with Trump, during the campaign or transition, had some form of communication with Russians. Thirteen Russian citizens, twelve Russian intelligence officials and three Russian companies have been charged with crimes in the Mueller probe. This is unprecedented. No other presidential campaign is believed to have ever knowingly contacted Russian agents, and the contacts were more than social.

• Paul Manafort attended a meeting in Trump Tower with Russians who claimed to have dirt on Hillary Clinton. He pleaded guilty to conspiracy against the United States and is also accused of sharing campaign data with Russian agents.
• Rick Gates, a senior campaign official, was in contact with Konstantin Klimnik, a Manafort business partner with suspected connections to Russian intelligence.

• Michael Flynn, former national security adviser, spoke on the phone with Russian Ambassador Sergey Kislyak and attended a meeting with the ambassador and Trump son-in-law Jared Kushner.

• Donald Trump Jr. attended a meeting with Russians at Trump Tower and met with other Russians.

• Kushner met with Kislyak and Russian banker Sergey Gorkov.

• George Papadopoulos, a campaign adviser, met with various Russians.

• Carter Page, a campaign adviser, met Kislyak during the Republican convention, Russian legislators and government-owned oil company Rosneft during trips to Moscow.

• Jeff Sessions, before appointment as attorney general, met with Kislyak at the Republican convention and again at his Senate office in Washington D.C.

• J.D. Gordon, a campaign official, met with Kislyak on at least two occasions.

• Roger Stone, a campaign adviser, met with Henry Greenberg, who offered dirt on Hillary Clinton and exchanged Twitter messages with Russian intelligence agents pretending to be a Russian hacker.

• Michael Caputo, a campaign aide, was also in touch with Greenberg and set up his meeting with Stone.

• Erik Prince, a Trump associate (founder of military contractor Blackwater and brother of Education Secretary Betsy DeVos), met with Russian banker Kirill Dmitriev during a trip to the Seychelles.

• Avi Berkowitz, Kushner's assistant, met with Kislyak during the transition.

• Michael Cohen, Trump's lawyer, spoke with at least two Russian companies during the campaign about building a Trump Tower in Moscow. Cohen, who pleaded guilty to tax fraud and campaign finance violations, promised to reveal further details about additional wrongdoing.

• Ivanka Trump, the president's daughter, contacted the wife of the Russian who offered "synergy" to Cohen.
• Felix Sater, a Trump business partner, spoke with Russians about a proposed Trump Tower in Moscow.

In January 2018, a Pew Research Center poll found that one-quarter of Republicans surveyed had a favorable view of Putin, while only 16 percent of Americans overall felt that way. Ironically, Obama left office with favorable ratings from only 10.7 percent of Republicans. The numbers are disturbing by showing that Republicans put more faith in Putin than Obama.

It's easy to understand why Americans admire statesmen like Nelson Mandela, Mikhail Gorbachev, Winston Churchill or Yitzhak Rabin, but esteem for Putin shows a dangerous sympathy for authoritarianism in the party that is running our government.

NATIONAL SECURITY

Perhaps the scariest thing about Trump is knowing that he is in charge of our nation's security, including the people he has entrusted with that sacred duty. Trump himself blurted out highly classified information to Russian Ambassador Sergei Kislyak and Russian Foreign Minister Sergey Lavarov during a White House meeting in May 2017, information so sensitive that it had not been shared with U.S. allies. The source for the intel about the Islamic State (ISIS) terrorist group did not grant permission for the United States to share it with anyone else. The president has the authority to declassify information, but this move was highly troubling and may have compromised sources.

Insiders disclosed that Trump shows scant interest in the "Presidential Daily Brief" meticulously assembled by experienced national security staff to prepare the president for a crisis that might erupt at any time. His predecessors devoured these detailed reports first thing in the morning. Not Trump. Instead of starting his day reading what the government's best-equipped security experts know about possible threats, Trump turns to his own brain trust, the blabbermouths on Fox News. As for the daily brief, he prefers to get a condensed version orally every few days.

In late January 2019, the "National Intelligence Strategy" warned that the United States faces a "toxic mix" of threats as its influence declines, giving Russia and China an opportunity to fill the gap. It contradicted Trump's statements in many areas. Dan Coats, director of National Intelligence, told the Senate Intelligence Committee: "We assess that foreign actors will view the 2020 U.S. elections as an opportunity to advance their interests." While Trump continues to pooh-pooh evidence of Russian interference in U.S. elections, this report said:

- "Traditional adversaries will continue attempts to gain and assert influence, taking advantage of changing conditions in the international environment – including the weakening of the post-WWII international order, increasingly isolationist tendencies in the West, and shifts in the global economy."
- Iran has not violated the 2015 nuclear agreement it made with Obama. This contradicts Trump's justification for jettisoning the painstakingly crafted deal.

• North Korea remains a nuclear threat. This counters Trump's remarks to have neutralized that nation's nuclear ambitions.
• Global climate change is a danger. This belies Trump's position that it is a hoax.
• Coats told the Senate, "ISIS is intent on resurging and still commands thousands of fighters in Iraq and Syria." Trump boasted that he had defeated the terrorist group.
• But the report declined to call the border with Mexico a crisis as Trump has said repeatedly and issued a National Emergency declaration to that effect.

Rather than acknowledging the accuracy of research by top security professionals, Trump called them "extremely passive and naive" and "perhaps intelligence should go back to school!" And it looks as if Coats' honesty and competence was too much for Trump, with rumors swirling that Coats is on his way out.

Trump instead trusted people like campaign chair Manafort and National Security Adviser Flynn with sensitive information, and they shared those details with adversaries. Donald Jr. met with a Russian agent. Federal intelligence specialists denied security clearances for at least thirty Trump appointees but, in an unprecedented move, were overruled by the White House. Instead of beefing up its security protocols, the Trump administration suspended Tricia Newbold, a White House security specialist, for refusing to approve top secret clearance for Jared Kushner. Furthermore, Trump revoked security clearances for numerous people for the sole reason that they criticized him; none was ever suspected compromising sensitive information. These people include former CIA

Director John Brennan, former FBI Director James Comey, former Director of National Intelligence James Clapper, former National Security Agency Director Michael Hayden, former national security adviser Susan Rice, former FBI attorney Lisa Page, former Deputy Attorney General Sally Yates, former FBI counterintelligence agent Peter Strzok, former FBI Deputy Director Andrew McCabe, and Bruce Ohr, who works in the Justice Department after being demoted from associate deputy attorney general. Not a peep out of Fox on this.

This is not only foolish, it is downright hazardous. Former presidents have faced withering criticism without yanking their critics' security clearances. Furthermore, most presidents have sought out predecessors and their top lieutenants for advice on weighty matters, notwithstanding party affiliation and political ideology. Trump is the first to ignore this tradition.

RESPECT OUR DIPLOMATS

When Rex Tillerson, the former CEO of ExxonMobil, took over the State Department from John Kerry, he had never worked in the public sector. He sought to reorganize America's diplomatic service along the lines of a corporation. But diplomats are not the same as wildcat drillers or refinery engineers, with a vastly different mission and skill sets. Tillerson was fired before he could remake the seventy-five-thousand-member department into a compliant corporate clone, but concerns still abound that Trump is damaging the department. All the senior-level managers retired before Tillerson arrived, part of the exodus of senior Foreign Service officers who refused to work for Trump. It was the biggest-ever hollowing out of experienced personnel in key positions.

Trump appointed a startling crew of unqualified people, from political hacks to campaign donors, as ambassadors. American emissaries to Germany, Israel and the Netherlands made outrageous statements that insulted the host governments. And still, more than two dozen ambassador's posts, as well as essential under-secretary positions, remained vacant after two years. Fortunately, veteran Jon Huntsman accepted the sensitive posting to Moscow. Huntsman, a Republican former governor of Utah, served previously as ambassador to China during the Obama administration and in Singapore before that.

Many career diplomats have expressed their displeasure over Trump's upheaval in foreign relations while unprecedented friction chafes our closest allies.

One diplomatic incident in particular should make Americans shiver. After a dozen Russian agents were indicted on charges of trying to hack the 2016 U.S. election, Putin offered Trump a deal at the July 2018 summit in Helsinki: U.S. agents could witness the questioning of the Russians (by Russian agents) if Trump allowed the Russians to interrogate Michael McFaul, the former U.S. Ambassador to Moscow. Trump naively blabbered that this as an "incredible offer," but experienced people saw through the ruse. Russian prosecutors had named McFaul, now a scholar at the Hoover Institution at

Stanford University in California, a "person of interest" in their accusations against Bill Browder, a British financier the Russians accuse of tax fraud.

"Putin is seeking to arrest a former ambassador. Please understand how outrageous this act is, discussed between our two presidents," McFaul said on Twitter in response. "I hope the White House corrects the record and denounces in categorical terms this ridiculous request from Putin. Not doing so creates moral equivalency between a legitimate U.S. indictment of Russian intelligence officers and a crazy, completely fabricated story invented by Putin."

When the U.S. Senate voted 98-0 that the government should not make any current or former government employee or diplomat available for interrogation by Russia, the White House flip-flopped and said Trump "disagrees" with Putin's proposal.

ATTACKING THE JUDICIARY

The judge assigned to oversee the fraud case against Trump University in San Diego was Gonzalo Curiel. Trump called Curiel a "hater" who was unfair to him because he is "Hispanic," because he is "Mexican" and so he probably does not like Trump's idea of building a wall between the United States and Mexico.

The for-profit Trump University offered courses in real estate but was not accredited for college courses. It shut down after numerous lawsuits alleging fraud which resulted in financial settlements with former students.

Curiel is not Mexican. He was born of Mexican ancestry in Indiana, where he attended college. He worked as a federal prosecutor in narcotics cases in San Diego before Obama appointed him to the bench. As a prosecutor, Curiel was at times put into protective custody by federal law enforcement because of threats by drug traffickers. He is a reputable and courageous jurist.

Curiel wasn't Trump's only target. When he disagreed with a federal judge who struck down his Muslim ban as unconstitutional, the president derisively referred to him as a "so-called judge."

On yet another occasion, Trump complained about a Ninth Circuit federal court ruling against him, saying it had "Obama judges," that it is "a disgrace" and mocked the "independent judiciary." Chief Justice John Roberts struck back: "We do not have Obama judges or Trump judges, Bush judges or Clinton judges," he said. "What we have is an extraordinary group of dedicated judges doing their level best to do equal right to those appearing before them."

Trump lackey Roger Stone posted on Instagram an ominous photo of U.S. District Judge Amy Berman Jackson, who is presiding over his trial for obstruction of justice and witness tampering, shown with a crosshairs looming overhead, alleging "legal trickery" by an "Obama appointed judge."

Intimidation of judges is unconscionable and irresponsible. An independent judiciary is a necessary hallmark that sets us apart from dictatorships.

DISSENT

The way a democracy deals with dissent is a testament to its strength and basic legitimacy. Free nations tolerate dissent. Dictatorships don't. Putin's Russia cracks heads when people take to the streets to make their voices heard. Look at pictures from Tiananmen Square for a glimpse at how China handles dissent. Venezuelans who demonstrate against the regime are shot. Protest is celebrated as a way of life in free countries like the United States and European democracies. But Trump's approach resembles Putin more than it does any of his predecessors.

Trump had a troubling pattern of encouraging violence against protesters who showed up at various rallies during the 2016 campaign. After Trump supporters punched and kicked a Black Lives Matter demonstrator on November 21, 2015 in Birmingham, Alabama, Trump said: "Maybe he should have been roughed up." In February 2016 amid protests at a rally in Cedar Rapids, Iowa, he told his supporters to "Knock the crap out of him, would you? I promise you, I will pay your legal fees." On February 23, 2016, he said of a demonstrator in Las Vegas: "I'd like to punch him in the face." At a March 2016 campaign stop in Warren, Michigan, where protesters were forcibly removed, Trump said: "If you do (hurt him), I'll defend

96

you in court, don't worry about it." When a protester tried to rush the stage at a campaign event on March 12, 2016 in Dayton, Ohio, Trump said: "I'll beat the crap out of you."

Trump denies it, but he is not the only liar. He encourages his staff to prevaricate on his behalf. "The president in no way, form, or fashion has ever promoted or encouraged violence," Press Secretary Sarah Huckabee Sanders said June 29, 2017 at the White House daily press briefing. She must keep "hear no evil, see no evil, speak no evil" voodoo dolls on her desk.

Presidents and candidates have vigorous Secret Service protection, so they are rarely in danger of bodily harm. Yes, loud protesters might upset candidates, but safety is rarely an issue (except when armed demonstrators frequently showed up at Obama events).

Trump even congratulated Congressman Greg Gianforte, who pleaded guilty to assaulting a reporter. Instead of condemning this crime, Trump said at an October 2018 rally in Montana: "Any guy that can do a body slam, he's my guy."

After Trump consistently defamed the news media and his political antagonists as "enemies of the people" it was inevitable that someone would act on these provocations. Coast Guard Lieutenant Paul Hasson, a self-identified Trump fan, was arrested in February 2019 with a cache of weapons, ammo, and a hit list of journalists and Democratic lawmakers to murder in his quest to form a "white homeland."

Obama took a different approach to dealing with malcontents.

At a November 4, 2016 rally in Fayetteville, North Carolina to promote Hillary Clinton's candidacy, a pro-Trump heckler interrupted Obama's speech. Instead of threatening violence, Obama tried to quiet those who were booing the man. "Hold up," Obama said repeatedly. "I told you to be focused, you're not focused right now." He then defended the protester, saying: "You've got an older gentleman who is supporting his candidate. He's not doing nothing. You don't have to worry about him. We live in a country that respects free speech."

After being heckled by several loud protesters at a November 25, 2016 speech in Chicago, Obama responded "I've been respectful" and pointed out that he did not order them removed. "I've heard you, but you've got to listen to me too. All right? I understand you may disagree, but we've got to be able to talk honestly about these issues."

Obama was not unique in dealing with dissent gracefully. Both Clintons and both Bushes reacted in a dignified manner. Again we must ask why we allow a president to behave in such a disgraceful way that breaks with centuries of tradition.

How will historians judge the different approaches to dissent by these two presidents? When we explain freedom of speech and basic civility to kids, which approach better expresses our values? When our children face adversity, do we encourage them to resort to violence or seek peaceful solutions whenever possible?

HEROES ARE HARD TO FIND

For most Americans, war heroes are the stuff of legend. Leading the Allied forces during the Second World War helped catapult Dwight Eisenhower into the White House the same way that Civil War General Ulysses Grant won the presidency a century earlier. And we can't forget that our first president, George Washington, was a general in the Revolutionary War. Stature as a Vietnam War hero helped propel John McCain to the Senate and to the Republican nomination for president in 2008. Obama, the grandson of a World War II veteran, running against McCain that year, praised the senator's war record while respectfully opposing his policy differences.

The Arizona senator was lauded by Republicans and Democrats but drew sneers from Trump. McCain, a fighter pilot, was shot down over North Vietnam and repeatedly beaten and tortured during his five years in captivity. "He's not a war hero," said Trump, who dodged the draft during the Vietnam War. "He was a war hero because he was captured. I like people who weren't captured."

Even as McCain's family was still mourning his death, Trump mocked the late senator in a lunch with TV news anchors before his State of the Union address in February 2019, saying: "By the way, he wrote a book, and the book bombed."

THE GOD SQUAD

Many people sympathize with the religious right's spiritual intentions but oppose their political agenda, outsize influence on government, and intolerance toward those who do not share their vision of God's design for mankind. Merging church and state is unsafe and destabilizing. Theocracies throughout history and around the world – in Yemen, Sudan, Saudi Arabia, Iran and Afghanistan – have a poor record of protecting the rights of religious minorities and freedom in general.

It's important to separate the leaders of these movements from the followers. Most of the religious faithful are well meaning and sincere, not zealots. Martin Luther King used the Bible to support racial equality, challenging the professed Christianity of his racist opponents (the Klan burns crosses, not Islamic crescents).

The rub is that extremists believe they hold the only truth and that this gives them license to force it on others. Why should this be any surprise? Our earliest settlers were the Pilgrims who fled religious persecution in Europe then turned around to burn accused "witches" at the stake. Fortunately, our founding fathers a century later were a diverse mix of believers and nonbelievers, with no single religious doctrine. Knowing about the abuses and excesses of government-mandated religiosity, these men of the Enlightenment saw it as a universal right to find one's own spiritual path without requiring it for others.

Nevertheless, some religious leaders assume it is their right to set the moral compass for everyone, and they persuade well-intended believers to follow along. They go so far as to claim that the United States was created as an official "Christian nation." It never was. In fact, the First Amendment of the Constitution says quite the opposite: "Congress shall make no law respecting an establishment of religion, or prohibiting the free exercise thereof."

For Trump, this is a sea of opportunity. He catered to the religious right by recruiting Mike Pence as vice president, winning over religious figures with their huge flocks. Pence has all the right credentials to excite this portion of the base. As a congressman and governor of Indiana, he obsessively fought any law to prevent discrimination based on sexual orientation and blocked access to contraception. His wife, Karen, teaches at a school which bans students and teachers who condone homosexuality. Under such criteria, their doorway would bar Pope Francis. When the pontiff was asked about taking confession from a gay person, he responded, "Who am I to judge?" The head of the world's 1.1 billion Roman Catholics explained "these people should be treated with delicacy and not be marginalized" and "people should not be defined only by their sexual tendencies." The Pence view is light years outside the mainstream. A 2018 Gallup poll showed 67 percent of Americans deem same-sex relationships acceptable, while 30 percent describe such relations as "morally wrong."

One of the great contradictions of our age is that the religious right has been indoctrinated to hate Obama, who by all accounts is a loyal Christian, and adore Trump, a serial adulterer and pretender who makes a mockery of faith. Trump's followers don't seem to care if he really believes anything he says; they just want authority to dictate the "morals" of others, a power that Obama denied them.

It appears not to matter if Trump cheated people in business, sexually molested women, was an adulterer, and bullies the disabled. Trump blatantly broke most of the Ten Commandments habitually except the sixth (there is no reason to believe he murders people).

It's also incongruous, and supremely troubling, that Trump's base is willing to follow him in demonizing desperate refugees from Central America, where the population is among the world's greatest concentration of their fellow Christians, most of them Catholic. Instead of Trump, perhaps they should follow the Bible, where Proverbs 14:31 says, "Whoever oppresses a poor man insults his Maker, but he who is generous to the needy honors him."

In the 1990s it was common for Christians to ask WWJD (What Would Jesus Do?) when they struggled with gnawing ethical questions. It seems like a sensible guideline for many people trying to do the right thing. So, shouldn't we pin down evangelicals about whether Jesus would pry terrified tots from their parents' arms and throw them into prison camps?

In the year I spent researching *The Obama Haters*, I found his most rabid critics prone to lying about him were religious crusaders in violation of the Ninth Commandment about not bearing false witness against your neighbor.

WHAT DO WE TELL THE CHILDREN?

The Reverend Franklin Graham, son of the late evangelist Billy Graham (who befriended presidents of both parties), said Obama is "against Christ and against his teachings." He trotted out the discredited slur of Obama being a Muslim and said his foreign policy was not in keeping with a Christian world view. Graham also called Islam a "very evil and wicked religion." It makes me wonder whether he has met any Muslims. In my travels around Turkey, Oman and the United Arab Emirates, I met hundreds of warm, gracious, welcoming people. Some were pious and others secular, as are members of any faith. Graham and Trump differ with President George W. Bush, who said, "Islam, as practiced by the vast majority of people, is a peaceful religion, a religion that respects others. Ours is a country based upon tolerance and we welcome people of all faiths in America." Graham also defended Trump after the affair with porn star Stormy Daniels (Stephanie Clifford), saying the president is a "changed man." He believes that "God put him (Trump) there (in the White House)." Trump's press secretary, Sarah Huckabee Sanders mimicked Graham in late January 2019, telling the Christian Broadcast Network that God "wanted Donald Trump to be president." God has yet to confirm whether Graham and Huckabee Sanders spoke on his behalf.

Televangelist Pat Robertson blamed Obama for school shootings because he allegedly allowed "witchcraft and lesbianism into the White House ... We turned our back on God and now we see evil school shootings." School shootings have been recorded in the United States since 1840, and Robertson never mentioned that such tragic incidents also occurred during the presidencies of Ronald Reagan, both Bushes, and Trump. The octogenarian preacher theorized that indictments of Trump administration officials were the result of an Obama-inspired conspiracy and that those opposing Trump are fighting against God. Even though Robertson is convinced that lesbians are somehow responsible for school shootings, it should be noted that both Bush Junior and Trump have been largely tolerant toward gays.

Pope Francis apparently did not let alleged White House witchcraft affect his warm relationship with Obama, who attended Catholic school while living in Indonesia as a child. In a 2004 interview with the *Chicago Sun-Times*, Obama described his "altar call" in affirming his Christian faith and emphasized, "I'm a big believer in tolerance. I think that religion at its best comes with a big dose of doubt. I'm suspicious of too much certainty in the pursuit of understanding just because I think people are limited in their understanding." He also said, "I am a big believer in the separation of church and state ... I am a great admirer of our founding charter and its resolve to prevent theocracies from forming and its resolve to prevent disruptive strains of fundamentalism from taking root in this country." Trump has never made any clear, soulful explanation about what faith means to him and how it relates to public life. He stumbles when referencing the Bible: He famously quoted "One Corinthians" instead of the correct "First Corinthians."

Lest we forget, at least three prominent Christian preachers publicly prayed for Obama's death during his time in office. The Obama-hating preachers are now Trump lovers.

RACISM

The Trump family was infamous for racism long before Donald Trump became a household word. Trump's father, Fred, was such a miserable landlord that America's iconic songwriter, Woody Guthrie, immortalized him in the 1950s with the lyrics "I suppose that Old Man Trump knows just how much racial hate/He stirred up in that bloodpot of human hearts/When he drawed that color line/Here at his Beach Haven family project...Beach Haven is Trump's Tower/Where no black folks come to roam."

These weren't just verses by a folk singer. In 1973, the Department of Justice sued the Trumps for housing discrimination. A former hotel executive said Trump told him, "Laziness is a trait in blacks." Trump famously bought newspaper ads to call for the death penalty for five black and Hispanic teenagers accused of raping a white woman in Central Park, even after they were exonerated by DNA evidence. Trump said Obama's policies to help legalize the status of the "dreamers," law-abiding immigrants brought to the United States illegally as infants, contributed to the spread of gang violence, with no evidence. He asserted that immigrants from Haiti "all have AIDS" and that Nigerians coming to the United States would never "go back to their huts." Trump asked lawmakers in an Oval Office meeting, "Why do we want all these people from 'shithole countries' coming here?" He was referring to nations with black citizens, saying, "Why do we need more Haitians? Take them out." Trump falsely claimed that Obama "issued a statement for Kwanzaa but failed to issue one for Christmas." He fails to condemn hate crimes committed by whites against minorities but is quick to clamor about any crime committed by a black or Hispanic. While claiming ignorance about white nationalists, he retweets their hate-mongering tweets. Trump urges that any professional football player who "takes a knee" during the National Anthem to protest racism be fired because he is "a disgrace" and "son of a bitch." Former White House adviser Omarosa Manigault Newman, a black woman, said she has a tape recording of Trump using racist language.

People of all races owe it to their kids to denounce racism by Trump or any other person.

MOLESTING WOMEN

A month before the election, a videotape surfaced in which Trump bragged about sexually assaulting women: "I'm automatically attracted to beautiful (women) – I just start kissing them. It's like a magnet. Just kiss. I don't even wait. And when you're a star they let you do it. You can do anything ... Grab them by the pussy. You can do anything."

It was impossible to deny, so Trump and his minions just made excuses, that it was "locker room banter" and "a private conversation that took place years ago." Locker room braggadocio might be excused for high school students, but the "Access Hollywood" tape was recorded in 2005, when Trump was fifty-nine! Many parents prohibit their teenagers from associating with other kids they hear talk like this; mine did. How can millions then vote for a president who behaves that way?

The great incongruity is that many people who now support Trump bitterly condemned Bill Clinton over a consensual affair. Conservatives said nonstop: "If he's not faithful to his wife, he can't be trusted to be faithful to this country." While the relationship with Monica Lewinsky was wrong on many levels, it was consensual, not forced. Grabbing genitalia, as Trump boasts about doing, constitutes sexual assault and is illegal in every jurisdiction of the United States.

Since the 1980s, at least nineteen women have accused Trump of sexual impropriety, including sexual assault, sexual harassment or groping. Then there were the lawsuits by porn actress Stormy Daniels (Stephanie Clifford) and Playboy model Karen McDougal, claiming that Trump representatives paid them off to keep silent. Who knows if other affairs might have been "settled" with nondisclosure agreements?

From the earliest grades in school, we educate youngsters about "inappropriate touching" to protect them. That touching is no less inappropriate when the assailant is the president.

MUSLIM BAN

While campaigning for president in December 2015, Trump endorsed a ban on all Muslims entering the United States, saying: "Donald J. Trump is calling for a total and complete shutdown of Muslims entering the United States until our country's representatives can figure out what is going on." The 911 hijackers were extremists following the orders of an evil fanatic who distorted Islam and terrorized innocent people. Al-Qaeda and ISIS are terrorist organizations notwithstanding any religious posturing, and their most frequent targets are other Muslims. By pushing for a ban on all Muslims, Trump reinforced the argument of radicals that moderate Muslims should not cooperate with outsiders because they will be hated no matter what. And it was a clear violation of the Constitution.

Trump did not succeed in banning all Muslims, but he issued Executive Order 13769 which prevents the entry into the United States of people born in Iran, Iraq, Libya, Somalia, Sudan, Syria and Yemen. This resulted in turning back travelers and revoking visas for people from those Muslim-majority countries. Fifteen of the nineteen hijackers on September 11 were from Saudi Arabia, where the government has financed schools and organizations which preach "jihad" against the West. In spite of this fact and the Saudi government's murder of Jamal Khashoggi, a U.S. resident, a journalist for *The Washington Post*, and prominent critic of his government, Trump remains a strong backer of the Saudi dictatorship. Trump defends the Saudis in purely transactional terms: they invest some of their oil wealth in the United States and supply oil. Some 911 hijackers also came from the United Arab Emirates, Egypt and Lebanon, but none of those countries ever suffered sanctions from Trump or any other U.S. administration. Trump is punishing citizens of countries which have not sent known terrorists to our soil and whose citizens may simply be escaping dangers at home. The result inflames mutual hatred.

Trump repeatedly says Muslims and Mexicans are menacing but never admits that white supremacists pose a terrorist threat. FBI Director Christopher Wray said the bureau had relatively the same number of open cases involving threats by white nationalists as by Islamic groups. "We take both of them very, very seriously," Wray told the Senate Homeland Security and Governmental Affairs Committee. "Our focus is on violence and threats of violence against the people of this country. That's our concern – it's not ideology." Timothy McVeigh, the New York-born terrorist who murdered 168 Americans in Oklahoma City on April 19, 1995, was a Catholic. We don't hear suggestions of sanctions against Catholics. The Ku Klux Klan calls itself a Christian organization, and its members are Protestants. They have killed countless innocent people. Why then are all Muslims tarred by the sins of Al-Qaeda and ISIS, while the Klan's evil deeds don't spill over to other Christians? We are told that Muslims are inherently threatening because they terrorize their own kind: Sunnis and Shiites kill each other. Christians have been doing the same thing in Ireland, where Catholics and Protestants have been murdering each other for a long, long time.

Muslims worship one God, as do Christians and Jews, simply with another name. People pray to Allah, Yahweh or Jehovah. Moses, Abraham, David, the Old Testament giants who represent so much to Christians and Jews ... they mean the same to Muslims. The Klan is a good starting point to explain

109

how some haters distort religion. The fact that the KKK burns crosses to terrorize people does not mean that they represent Christianity. The world is full of so many beliefs, such as Buddhists, Hindus, Jains, and Bahá'í that we must prepare curious kids for the varieties they will encounter.

IMMIGRATION

I suppose many of us are hypocrites in one way or the other. That's human nature. But Trump could win a gold medal in that category for his attitude toward immigration, both legal and illegal, for what he labels "chain migration." That refers to the U.S. guideline for "family reunification" which grants preference to people who petition for residency for spouses, parents, children and other family members. Trump calls the policy a national security threat.

He didn't seem to think it was a threat when Melania, who was born in Slovenia, sponsored her parents to become legal residents, allowing them to later take the oath as citizens in 2018. But Trump's backers never question him about his own family's "chain migration."

Don't forget that numerous Trump businesses have been caught employing undocumented aliens. Furthermore, it bears emphasizing that during the spring of 2018 Trump's "zero tolerance" policy ordered immigration officials to forcibly separate children from parents of refugees. Only when the public outcry reached a deafening howl did the administration backtrack. First, they claimed that the policy was not intentional, until ground-level people inside the government admitted it was. Then they tried to blame Obama, saying it was a carry-over of his policies. More cock and bull. Yes, it did happen occasionally during previous administrations, but it was not stated policy to take children away from their parents unless human trafficking or child abuse was apparent. Trump snatched untold thousands of youngsters away from their parents and put them in prison camps. Two children died in detention. By early 2019, no one even knew how many families had been reunited.

In a curious turn of events, some of those children were placed in a makeshift prison camp in Texas called Tornillo. The word *tornillo* in Spanish, fittingly, means "screw." You can't make this stuff up.

If a hostile government was doing to migrant children what Trump did, Americans would scream of kidnap, child abuse and human trafficking and might even back an invasion. Children who watch the news must be especially sensitive to images of youngsters yanked from mothers' arms and carted away. How can self-proclaimed "family values" advocates in Trump's base continue to make excuses for him and this immoral policy?

Perhaps we should all heed the words of Franklin Delano Roosevelt: "A nation does not have to be cruel to be tough."

THE WELCOME MAT

The world has changed a great deal since I grew up in the sixties. Racial and cultural minorities have made huge advances in claiming their rightful slice of the American pie, but not without major backlash. Japanese were put into internment camps during the Second World War. Even some Caucasians had to fight for their rights. When my parents were younger, some landlords and employers posted signs saying "No Irish" or "No Italians." Thank goodness most Americans now reject all that narrow-mindedness and value inclusiveness. Children from other countries go through immersion in English to fit in as soon as possible. Our country has long shown pride as a "melting pot." Coins and paper currency are stamped with our national motto, the Latin E PLURIBUS UNUM, which means "out of many, one." Ignoring the best of our traditions and conjuring up our most shameful tendencies from the past, Trump vilifies immigrants. Have we yanked away the welcome mat from the Statue of Liberty, which embraces newcomers with the stirring appeal: "Give me your tired, your poor, your huddled masses?"

TEACH YOUR CHILDREN WELL

Aristotle said, "Educating the mind, without educating the heart, is no education at all." His words remain true today, two millennia later. Education is vital for the mind and heart. By educating the heart, we teach children to do the right thing.

WHAT DO WE TELL THE CHILDREN?

Teachers have one of the most important and demanding jobs in the world.

In the Trump era, their work has become infinitely more difficult. What can a civics teacher tell a snickering junior high school class when asked about a president who cheated on all three wives with mistresses, including a pornographic actress and a Playboy model? What about his bullying of the weak, denigrating heroes, and taking immigrant children away from their parents? What if they ask whether the media are the "enemy of the people" or FBI investigators are thugs? In countless examples, Trump's behavior contradicts the values students learn at home and in school. And an honest answer by a teacher could bring a mob of parents storming the office of the school board or principal. The only safe option is to turn it back to the students and let them discuss it while playing the role of an impartial debate moderator.

So the question ricochets throughout this book: What do we tell the next generation about the behavior of a rogue president? Youth comprise our most important constituency. If they accept Trump's conduct as normal, their view of democracy and the world may be warped, perhaps permanently damaged. They risk becoming a generation of cynics, distrusting a system that gave rise to a president who shows that winning by any means is all that counts. After an endless barrage of crudeness, incivility and lies from this president, we are in danger of refusing to believe his successor, even if he or she is eminently truthful. Students and others could view our political crisis as merely a partisan food fight rather than what it truly is: a decisive battle for the heart and soul of America.

Quoting Aristotle, we should ask whether Trump's mind and heart were ever educated. The same question could be asked about Donald Jr., who, during a February 11, 2019 speech in El Paso, took this chilling swipe at educators: "You don't have to be indoctrinated by these loser teachers that are trying to sell you on socialism from birth."

In Chapter 2, Steven Levitsky and Daniel Ziblatt's *How Democracies Die* showed how Trump is destabilizing democracy through attacks on political opponents, courts, law enforcement and the media. The newest insidious salvo against teachers is another perilous step in that direction, a full-throated attempt to topple one of the pillars of a free society. When dictators take power, they jail political opponents, independent judiciary, journalists and educators. It's even more frightening that this assault comes from Donald Jr., suggesting that a demagogue's son believes he has the power of a hereditary monarch.

Does Trump's administration have any interest in teaching our students? Franklin Delano Roosevelt called education "the safeguard of our democracy." While the right to a free public education is a bedrock principle in our country, it is no longer a priority. Betsy DeVos, married to an heir to the Amuay fortune, was appointed education secretary after her vociferous advocacy for vouchers, which are government subsidies for private schools that divert badly needed funding from public schools. Ninety percent of American students attend public primary and secondary schools, while the rest go to private schools, three-quarters of them religious institutions. When DeVos took office, she had to go on a learning tour because she knew almost nothing about public schools. And that was just the start. She made it her mission to reverse Obama's crackdown on for-profit higher education that saddles students with debt without teaching marketable skills (ever heard of Trump University?). DeVos reversed regulations that made it harder for such diploma mills to prey on students and reinstated an accreditation agency which had given passing grades to institutions so bad that they closed down. And here's her *coup de grâce*: The Obama administration had a program of loan forgiveness for students who had incurred crippling debt from these scams. Instead of clamping down on the swindlers, DeVos one upped Ebenzer Scrooge by squeezing students who had been cheated to make them pay back their loans.

CASABLANCA MOMENT

We could be hurtling toward an eventual *Casablanca* moment in which Republican leaders and other Trump supporters, one by one, finally prove themselves to be the equivalent of commie *apparatchiks*, dupes and sycophants in a Stalinist state. When the truth finally gushes out about Trump's misdeeds, either before or after he leaves office, his most ardent apologists will pretend they knew nothing about any of it, even though the rest of us clearly saw it. They will sound like Claude Rains' character Captain Renault in the classic film who shuts down the café owned by Rick, played by Humphrey Bogart, when he scolds "I'm shocked, shocked, to find that gambling is going on in here" as he pockets his own winnings.

8

SOLUTIONS: A PLAN OF ACTION

The time is always right to do what is right

–Martin Luther King Jr.

OUR CHALLENGE AHEAD

U P TO NOW I have described, as fairly and accurately as I can, the harm Donald Trump and his administration are inflicting on our country, how he has turned his back on our democratic traditions and how his behavior threatens our national security. For those who voted against him, there is no "I told you so" satisfaction. Our challenge is far too serious and too urgent for partisan squabbling. I remember Martin Luther King Jr.'s words: "I believe that unarmed truth and unconditional love will have the final word." He gave everything, including his life, to improve the world for people he never met. We owe it to Dr. King and others who made their sacrifices on our behalf to carry on, to not let their travails be in vain. We must decide how we will proceed. This chapter presents practical suggestions for people of all political perspectives to help us move together toward a better tomorrow. It won't be easy, and it won't happen overnight. We cannot surrender, and we cannot seek refuge in a democratic haven like Canada or Scandinavia. We must stand our ground and fight for what is ours.

SOMETHING TO UNITE AGAINST

Trump's greatest success as president, ironically, is to have united people of all ages, genders, income levels, education, political views, religions and professions AGAINST what he is doing. He created the catapult upon which the opposition is rising. That's been clear since Inauguration Day, which energized the most widespread protests in U.S. history. At least four million people participated in the peaceful Women's March in all fifty states.

During Barack Obama's presidency, people protested loudly, but many were misinformed citizens misled by false claims: that he was a Muslim, born in Kenya, a Communist, or even more absurd fantasies like health insurance "death panels" or sending political opponents to be imprisoned in "FEMA Camps," with no link to reality. And let's face it, some critics were outright racists who later marched in white nationalist demonstrations that Trump condoned. The anti-Obama protests, while attention grabbing, never reached massive numbers or came close to representing a cross-section of Americans.

The perverse policies of Trump and his henchman have galvanized people who previously were not politically active. Many new members of Congress after the 2018 midterm elections were neophytes who felt motivated to enter politics to oppose the Trump agenda and get rid of anyone who served as a loyal enabler. They included women, Hispanics, African-Americans and Native Americans who were outraged by Trump's conduct and policies they considered sexist or racist. Trump not only drove new faces and ideas into the opposition but also exposed many things that were going wrong below the radar, such as voter suppression, gerrymandering, and undue influence by lobbyists.

Trump's candidacy and election emboldened white supremacists. This, in turn, propelled opponents of racism to stage counter-protests. The most prominent among those incidents occurred in August 2017 at the "unite the right" rally by white nationalists on the University of Virginia campus in Charlottesville to protest removal of a Confederate monument. Some marchers chanted "blood and soil," the slogan used by Nazis suggesting that ethnicity is based only on blood descent, and hoisted flags with Nazi symbols. Counter-protesters showed up, and violent clashes ensued. White supremacist James Alex Fields intentionally rammed his car into counter-protesters, killing Heather Hayer and injuring nineteen others. Trump blamed both sides for the violence, emphasizing that there were "very fine people" among both the white supremacists and counter-protesters. Obama responded on Twitter with a line from Nelson Mandela: "No one is born hating another person because of the color of his skin or his background or his religion." With more than 3.3 million likes and 1.3 million retweets, it became the most-liked tweet ever on Twitter. Later Obama chided Trump, saying: "How hard can that be? Saying that Nazis are bad."

Obama and others have thrown down the gauntlet. We must pick it up, march forward and not silently allow one man to undermine our traditions and our future.

LEGISLATIVE AND LEGAL REMEDIES

Chapter 3 explored gerrymandering and voter suppression. We need to work at all levels – local, state and national – to insure our constitutional right to "one person, one vote" and avoid these pitfalls. Independent commissions should draw lines for congressional districts based on accurately expressing the will of the people rather than allowing one party to seize unrepresentative power at the expense of the other. As for voter suppression, it will only end with massive mobilization. If one party is pushing anti-democratic rules, those must be challenged in court and its elected representatives turned out of office. Paper ballots and audits would help to guarantee the integrity of vote counts; efforts to move this proposal through Congress have met with resistance.

After Trump took a meat cleaver to chop away large sections of two national monuments in Utah, it highlighted the urgency for Congress to protect remaining national monuments from future pilfering. National monuments belong to all of us and future generations. They are not the property of Trump of any other president to give away to the highest bidder.

The longest federal government shutdown in history occurred under Trump from December 2018 to late January 2019, forcing the furlough of eight hundred thousand workers.

Trump, his family and administration showed callousness to the suffering of workers who missed two paychecks, putting them at risk of eviction and unable to pay for food and medicine. All we heard from the privileged Trump circle was "let them eat cake" remarks. To avert a shutdown, Congress had reached a government funding deal with Trump, but he backed out after taking heat from right-wing commentators. The loss of billions of dollars to the U.S. economy, undeserved suffering of government employees and contractors, and safety hazards due to absenteeism of indispensable people like air-traffic control workers make it clear that this must not be allowed again.

LIMITS ON LOBBYING

Some of the most troubling accusations against Trump and people around him involve influence peddling by governments hostile to American interests. His advisers who had received money from Russia and Turkey recommended favorable treatment for those governments. This was something Obama had prevented in his own administration by executive order. When Trump supporters yelled "drain the swamp" they were woefully unaware that Trump had no intention of putting it into practice.

It's not only Russian influence. Cabinet secretaries oversee sectors for which they had lobbied until recently or which have a direct impact on their own investment portfolios.

Executive Order 13490 was an ethics pledge signed the day after Obama took the oath of office. It banned gifts from lobbyists, prevented officials from participating in decisions which affect former employers for at least two years, prevented work as a lobbyist for at least two years, and other strict conflict-of-interest rules. But Trump modified the order to weaken the revolving-door provisions.

Sadly, we see how a transparent policy by one president can be ignored or demolished by the next. Therefore, it's clear that we need to codify such practices. If someone decides to lobby on behalf of a foreign government, they've made their choice, for whatever reason. Going to work for the U.S. government becomes an instant conflict of interest. A large part of Robert Mueller's probe involves what Paul Manafort, Michael Flynn and others did on behalf of their foreign clients while working for the Trump campaign or administration. This predicament should never even arise. Someone who has ever lobbied for a foreign state should be forbidden from holding a position of influence in the U.S. government. This is not a partisan issue. People of all political ideologies must agree that loyalty to the United States is the first and foremost duty of anyone holding elective or appointed office. After what has happened involving Trump associates, effective regulations to prevent this from happening again should be a top priority for Congress.

TAX RETURNS

Trump was the first president in decades to not share his tax returns with the public. We all have a right to know the sources of income and possible conflicts of interest of a potential president or vice president. A whiff of impropriety swirls around Trump's business activities. Does he cheat on his taxes? Did he swindle contractors and subcontractors for his projects? Has he done business with or obtained loans from unsavory characters who might influence his decisions? Complete tax returns would answer a lot of those questions. If presidential aspirants refuse to be candid about their finances, what are they hiding? These worries could be cast aside by financial transparency requirements, and refusal to comply should warrant instant disqualification. We need to pressure Congress to make this simple gesture compulsory.

In late January 2019, Democrats introduced the "For the People Act" which would require presidential candidates to release their tax returns and super PACs (political action committees) to disclose donors who contribute more than ten thousand dollars. Boatloads of secret money is clearly anti-democratic, but Senate Majority Leader Mitch McConnell vowed to sink the legislation he called "a power grab." He was right. It is a power grab – by the American people, to take back the power seized by deep-pocket special interests that fund his party's campaigns. We need take this directly to our elected representatives and demand common-sense reforms.

ELECTORAL COLLEGE

Hillary Clinton won 65,844,610 votes, or 48.2 percent of the total, to Trump's 62,979,636, or 46.1 percent. It was the fifth time in U.S. history that the candidate who came in second was sworn in as president. In a popular election, the candidate who gets the most votes should be the winner. This is obvious, not a loser's sour grapes. In a true democracy, the winner should take office every time, not just most of the time. Trump said afterward that if the election were decided by the popular vote, he would have spent more time in places like California and Texas and won anyway. But in that scenario, Hillary also could have swung voters, and the margin would have been pretty much the same.

Merriam-Webster's Dictionary defines democracy like this: "government by the people especially: rule of the majority." The electoral system does an injustice when it takes power from the hands of the candidate chosen by the will of the people. Congressman George Campbell, an ally of Thomas Jefferson, said: "In all free governments the will of the majority must be considered by the governments as the will of the nation." If our electoral system doesn't reflect the national will, perhaps it requires modification to avoid another travesty. Does anyone believe that our nation's founders intended for the second-place finisher to lead the country, not just once, but five times?

If we really want a democracy that reflects the views of the majority, we need to work tirelessly toward that purpose.

A PLAN OF ACTION

Scrapping the electoral college would take a constitutional amendment, a nearly impossible feat because states with smaller populations fear a loss of their outsize power. However, proposals have been made at the state level to reform the electoral college in a way that allows the popular vote winner to also capture the electoral college. After all, who among us knows the electors in our electoral college? Strangely, they are not even bound by law to vote for the winning candidate in their state. There were seven "faithless electors" in the 2016 presidential race who voted for neither Trump nor Hillary, but instead cast ballots for Bernie Sanders, Ron Paul, John Kasich, Colin Powell, and even Faith Spotted Eagle (who?) as well as people who were not on the ballot for vice-president. Such stunts make a mockery of the process, and perhaps those electors cast their votes this way to prove how irrational the entire system is.

I'd love to agree with Obama when he says "every vote counts." But does your vote really count when rogue electors disrespect the will of the people?

A concerted effort by people of all political views could help bring the electoral college into the twenty-first century. Again, this is where we the citizens need to flex our muscles and make our elected representatives listen, especially at the state level.

ACTIVISM

Things won't fix themselves if we just sit around and complain. This is not a matter of partisan politics. It is incumbent upon all of us to pressure political leaders to stand up for the traditional values upon which our nation has moved forward for more than two centuries. Instead, many politicians are controlled by big donors or fear primary challengers in gerrymandered districts that enhance the sway of the most extreme voices. If you want to get involved, there are countless non-government organizations that encourage public office holders to do the right thing. For a list of groups you could join as a member, volunteer or donate to further the cause of good government, see Appendix C.

Go to a town meeting held by your elected representative with friends and neighbors. Take your children; it's a great lesson in participatory democracy. Everyone can line up at the mike and ask a different question. Be respectful. Don't shout. Don't heckle. That only gives them the excuse to say your side is wrong. But don't let them double talk. If they change the topic or don't answer the question, ask again. "Excuse me, but you didn't answer my question. Let me rephrase it."

Be informed. Research your representative's past statements and positions so you can challenge him or her on specific points. If they have voiced support for Trump, make them defend it. If they have made any questionable statements, ask them what they meant. They are your elected representatives; don't let them get away with weasel words.

Don't let them get off without answering. You are in a majority. Remember that polls show most Americans don't like Trump.

If your member of Congress or Senate does not hold town meetings, confront him or her politely at public appearances. If they never appear in public, go to their district offices and demand that they be accountable to their constituents. If they still remain in hiding, contact news media in their district and force them to appear before the voters. We pay their salaries. They are accountable to us, not special interests and donors.

Don't forget local officeholders. Remember that some state legislatures gerrymandered their congressional districts to give Republicans lopsided representation. Make sure that your state is not allowed to do that, or if it has, work to fix it. Your state representative should also hold town hall meetings.

Here are some ideas for sample questions:

• Do you teach your children/grandchildren (as the case may be) that Donald Trump is a good role model? Why yes or no?

• Is it appropriate for the leader of our country to grab the genitalia of women as Trump has said he is proud of doing? Do you approve of his adultery with a porn star, Playboy model and at least nineteen women who have sued him? If it was wrong for Bill Clinton, how can it be right now?

• Do you think the American people have a right to see the tax returns of their president? Do you support the "For the People Act?" If not, why not?

• Do you support our National Parks and Monuments? If so, what did you do to prevent the giveaway of Bears Ears and Escalante National Monuments to energy companies?

• Do you believe it is humane to take infants away from their refugee parents? If not, what have you done to return those children to their parents? Do you support a president who is intentionally cruel to kids? Two children have died in U.S. custody. Do you want to continue this policy?

• Do you believe in strong law enforcement? If so, have you protested when Trump vilified people like Robert Mueller, the FBI, James Comey and Rob Rosenstein? Do you agree with Trump's description of federal agents as "thugs" and the Mueller investigation as a "witch hunt" despite Attorney General Bill Barr's sworn testimony to the contrary?

• Is it the government's job to protect the environment? If so, what did you do when Trump overturned laws to allow coal slurry to be dumped in public waterways, weakened environmental regulations and put unqualified men with conflicts of interest in charge of the Interior Department and EPA?

• Do you believe Donald Trump when he says Vladimir Putin did not meddle in our elections, or all the security agencies in our government who have concluded otherwise?

• Do you support a president who praises criminals like Paul Manafort and Michael Flynn who have confessed to serious crimes that endanger national security? If so, why?

• Do you believe gerrymandering reflects the will of the people? If not, have you stood up to protest against this patently undemocratic practice?

• Do you support Donald Trump's use of the description "Crooked Hillary" and continuing to encourage his crowds to chant "Lock Her Up?" Congress investigated her for years, through the end of 2018, and never found a crime. What crime did she commit, and why did Congress fail to uncover it after countless investigations and millions of dollars?

• Did you support Mitch McConnell denying a hearing for Merrick Garland's nomination as Supreme Court justice? McConnell said the American people should decide. A clear majority of Americans voted for Obama, who had the right to appoint a justice. In what way was McConnell's tactic consistent with over two hundred years of tradition? Was it democratic?

• Trump has said that support for NATO members should be dependent on dues they pay, and he has equivocated on support for countries such as the Baltic nations and Montenegro. Do you believe this makes NATO stronger in the eyes of potential adversaries?

• Trump has proposed U.S. withdrawal from NATO. Would you support such a move? Do you believe that someone who wants to pull out of NATO is suitable to lead our country?

• Do you agree with Trump that there were good people on both sides of the white supremacist march in Charlottesville that ended in the death of an innocent counter-protester?

• Do you agree that Trump should encourage violence against protesters at his rallies? Did you know that he told crowds to beat up protesters on numerous occasions? Do you encourage this kind of violence at your appearances? Have you ever spoken out against this?

• Scientists who study climate are almost unanimous in their conclusions that human activity causes climate change. Energy industry shills and Trump say global warming is a hoax. Which side do you believe and why?

• How do you believe American heroes should be treated? John McCain served our country as a fighter pilot and was tortured as a prisoner of war in North Vietnam for five years. Donald Trump is a draft dodger who says McCain was not a hero because he was captured. Do you support a draft dodger who treats American heroes with such disrespect?

• Trump said that American jobs would stop going overseas if he won. During the first year of his term, the Department of Labor showed 93,000 jobs were lost to outsourcing or trade competition. United Technologies and General Motors moved thousands of jobs overseas despite Trump's so-called deals. Do you support a president who fails to support American workers?

• Trump promised to balance the federal budget quickly. Instead, the deficit has ballooned since he took office, while Obama reduced the deficit in six out of his eight years in office. Do you support this growing deficit? Did you vote for the tax bill responsible for increasing the deficit?

• Do you support voter suppression that has led to reduced voter turnout of minorities in numerous states? (Look up the details in your own state or a nearby state for particulars).

• Do you believe it is good for democracy to have unlimited secret contributions by big donors? Do you support the "For the People Act?" If not, why not? Do you agree with the Citizens United decision that big money is the same thing as free speech?

POLITICAL ACTION

That's just the start. You know the local issues in your own state, so you can supplement this list with pointed questions of concern to local citizens. If you live in Kentucky, for instance, McConnell has a lot to answer for and should be grilled by residents every time he shows his face in public.

If you go in a group, you can record each other with cell phones asking questions and the responses of your representative. You just might cause them to make news by saying something outrageous or defending an untenable position. Indefensible remarks and positions need to be exposed. Share your recordings with local TV and radio stations, newspapers, blogs, anyone who can help you get the word out. Remember Mitt Romney did not know he was being recorded when he made his famous "47 percent" gaffe. If enough people get involved, the next election can be an even bigger blowout than the 2018 midterms.

What's important is to make sure that our representatives, whatever their party affiliation or political philosophy, support decency and democracy and actively endeavor to end the schemes that corrode our ideals. Trump has shown what happens when indecency and dishonesty go wild.

Rumors abound that some Republicans might challenge Trump for his party's nomination. Democrats have more than a dozen serious contenders, among them current or former governors, senators, congressional representatives, Cabinet secretaries, mayors, and possibly even a former vice president.

After political newcomer Obama vanquished the "inevitable" Hillary Clinton in 2008, Democrats with shorter résumés feel that they stand a chance. Following Trump's win with zero political experience, outsiders have reason to believe they might prevail with the right message. Sixty-plus percent of the population want to be rid of Trump. That means getting involved to help a qualified candidate defeat him. Just when many of us thought our country was lost, we now see that we have a legitimate chance to regain the independence from tyranny that our ancestors fought for in the Revolutionary War. The struggle won't be easy. Trump has the power of the office, big money behind him and a propaganda machine, including an influential TV network, ready to savage all rivals. Anyone who steps forward will face a meat grinder. Look at how Trump was able to overcome a stable full of experienced Republican contenders and then Hillary Clinton, with a mile-long résumé.

As author and radio host Thom Hartmann says, "Democracy is not a spectator sport. Tag, you're it!"

POSTSCRIPT

The Next Step: It's Up to Us to Restore Dignity and Decency

Have you no sense of decency?

–Joseph Welch

E very day something new shakes the world, often through the megaphone of a sharply worded Trump missive on Twitter. News organizations compile his prevarications by the thousands. Russian trolls disseminate disinformation believed by Trump fans rather than the facts compiled and meticulously verified by news organizations.

Close to 40 percent of Americans back Trump. He has declared war on the facts and truth. Despite better access to more information than ever, millions of people are woefully misinformed. *The Washington Post* has a new slogan "Democracy Dies in Darkness" attributed to Thomas Jefferson. A proverbial saying goes like this: "It's better to light a candle than curse the darkness." That's a start, but it's easier said than done.

Demagoguery is a problem as old as democracy itself and can only take root when we allow it. Informed people reject demagogues. Shakespeare seized upon the theme in *Julius*

Caesar, when Cassius told Brutus: "The fault, dear Brutus, is not in our stars. But in ourselves, that we are underlings." Caustic journalist H.L. Mencken put it more bluntly, saying: "The demagogue is one who preaches doctrines he knows to be untrue to men he knows to be idiots."

More than a third of the population can't be idiots, so how can so many people be harnessed to untrue versions of reality? It boils down to this: demagogues message through emotion, not facts. And, it helps to have a TV network which works tirelessly to brainwash people. So truth tellers must find more effective ways to reach that audience.

Fact-checking organizations exist for the sole purpose of sorting information. Appendix A contains tips for determining the veracity of information quickly and accurately. To help, there are comprehensive search engines like Google and Bing.

Since Trump rode down the escalator and declared his candidacy by exploiting hateful stereotypes to attack Hispanics, it is baffling to see how so many people can support someone whose statements and actions directly contradict their own professed beliefs. Something is wrong here, and it is unsettling.

Andrew McCabe, who rose through the FBI ranks before Trump fired him as acting director, described as "earth shattering" the president's willingness to believe Vladimir Putin more than America's own intelligence services and that Trump's relationship with Putin is "not typical." Even though experts have concluded that Russia meddled in the 2016 elections, the Trump administration is making little effort to combat further Russian cyber attacks leading up to the 2020 vote.

As a nation we are wandering through perilous uncharted territory. We have a president who is woefully unprofessional who hires people who are either incompetent or extremist ideologues unfit for the mission of their office. Trump shows so many signs of emotional instability that Washington has been abuzz with chatter about invoking the Twenty-Fifth Amendment, which allows removal of a president for incapacity. He is under investigation by the FBI for suspicion of conspiring with a hostile power, Russia, to influence our government. We went through some of this before with Richard Nixon, without the foreign connection, but at least he was prepared for the office after decades as vice president, senator and congressman. Trump is the least equipped and least qualified person to ever occupy the Oval Office.

So we must proceed with caution on many fronts simultaneously. If Trump leaves office before his term ends, Vice President Mike Pence would replace him. Pence knows how to pull the levers of power after years in Congress and as governor of Indiana. But there is so much potential illegality under investigation, we must be sure that Pence was not involved. There is no indication yet that Pence has done anything illegal, but at this crossroads in our history, we need to know for sure.

Before Nixon resigned, Vice President Spiro Agnew was forced out after conviction for tax fraud and bribery. Had Agnew ascended to the presidency, our national crisis would have been doubled with the resignations of two presidents in short order. Luckily, squeaky clean Gerald Ford was approved as vice president and steadied the ship of state when Nixon left in disgrace, telling the country "our long national nightmare is over."

Were Pence to exit the stage unexpectedly, Republicans would be anxious to replace him quickly because without a vice president, Democratic Speaker of the House Nancy Pelosi, whom Republicans loathe, would be next in line. In this event, Democrats would have to proceed very carefully because elevating Pelosi to the presidency would give license to right-wing conspiracy theories about plots against Trump. A replacement would require approval by both houses of Congress. Democrats now in charge of the House of Representatives would never approve a hyper-partisan Republican, and Republicans in the Senate would likewise not allow a fiercely partisan Democrat. The only choice would be someone of proven integrity and vast experience who could win the trust of the nation and the support of working majorities in each party. Few people in public life meet these criteria, but a handful of moderates from both parties with crossover appeal come to mind: former Maine Senator Olympia Snowe, a Republican; former Indiana Senator Evan Bayh and former Nebraska Senator Bob Kerrey, both Democrats; and former Rhode Island Senator and Governor Lincoln Chafee, a hybrid who has been elected to office by both major parties.

Can we allow Trump's behavior to become the norm? Do we deserve a president who lies so much? We do if we are unwilling to challenge what is wrong. Do we want a narcissistic bully instead of a bully pulpit? Do we want a leader who scoffs at protecting the environment, worker rights, and health and safety regulations? Do we want to be led by someone who cozies up to strongmen while treating democratic allies with disdain? Can we tolerate a president who abides racists while treating minorities with contempt? And finally, how can we trust a leader who thinks only of his own self interest while ignoring the needs of our nation? The choice is ours, and it is stark. Trump and his allies perilously destabilize our democracy. It's up to us to use democratic means to restore our heritage before it's too late.

The sad truth is that removing Trump, whether by election in 2020, impeachment and conviction, or resignation, will not solve our problem. The next president will face a huge challenge to govern because of obstruction by millions of revanchists. No matter how Trump leaves office, Fox News and the right wing will likely say he was railroaded by a "witch hunt."

As for impeachment, Democratic leaders are proceeding cautiously and responsibly. Jerrold Nadler of New York, chairman of the House Judiciary Committee, said that such an extreme step should be taken only "against a president who would aggrandize power, destroy liberty, destroy democratic institutions, destroy the separations of power." He emphasized that Democrats will not impeach Trump over "sexual McCarthyism" as the Republicans did to Bill Clinton. Pelosi also discourages talk about impeachment.

Unless and until the Republican Party rejects Trump's tactics, there is no clear way forward. Al Gore and Hillary Clinton bowed out gracefully even after they won the popular vote because they valued national unity more than their own ambitions.

Republican Party leaders must be equally patriotic, even if it means losing personal power. That means accepting a step down from the nearly unlimited power they had when they held the White House, both houses of Congress and a working majority on the Supreme Court.

It wasn't so long ago when Republican presidents, instead of deepening the wounds in the national psyche, sought to emphasize the positive, while preaching tolerance and unity. Ronald Reagan said, "If you love our country, you should also love our countrymen." Isn't that kind of sunny outlook what Americans truly want in a leader?

Getting rid of Trump is just a start. Our nation urgently needs both political parties to find common ground in what unites us. And that is hard to imagine when one-third of the population is willing to continue believing so many things that are certifiably false.

We must all grasp that Trump is not normal, that nothing he is doing is typical, that we risk the very future of our nation, our freedom and our traditions by allowing his behavior to become acceptable.

Trump's colossal failures were on full display at the fifty-fifth annual Munich Security Conference in February 2019 when US allies sat on their hands for Pence's recitation of Trump's talking points. They later applauded when his predecessor, Joe Biden, reaffirmed US commitment to NATO and international cooperation in a post-Trump world.

Democratic California Congressman Adam Schiff wrote in an opinion piece published February 21, 2019 in *The Washington Post* directed as his Republican colleagues: "Many of you have acknowledged your deep misgivings about the president in quiet conversations over the past two years. You have bemoaned his lack of decency, character and integrity. You have deplored his fundamental inability to tell the truth. But for reasons that are all too easy to comprehend, you have chosen to keep your misgivings and your rising alarm private. That must end. The time for silent disagreement is over. You must speak out."

Abraham Lincoln said, "Nearly all men can stand adversity, but if you want to test a man's character, give him power." Trump has shown in every instance that he has a frightening absence of integrity and is a serial abuser of his power.

Some political leaders recognize the enormity of what we confront and see our actions today through the prism of history. California Senator Kamala Harris told MSNBC on January 24, 2019: "Years from now, members of our family, our children and grandchildren, they're going to ask, 'Where were you at that inflection moment?'" She is a Democratic candidate for president.

Maryland Congressman Elijah Cummings, also a Democrat, told Congress on February 6, 2019: "I want to be clear that when they look back on this moment two hundred years from now, that there are those of us who stood up, and they'll be able to say they stood up and say they defended the right to vote."

Michigan Democratic Congressman Dan Kildee said he tells his Republican colleagues to "take a long view of history" when assessing Trump's behavior.

This profound sense of history is sorely lacking in our public discourse.

From the beginning, our republic has tolerated fringes. It is the duty of the mainstream, however, to challenge and push the extremists to the sidelines where they belong rather than mimic or silence them. Like a spoiled child throwing a tantrum, they should be ignored and not given center stage. Future generations will judge us negatively if fringe elements further damage our institutions. Americans look back on the stain of slavery and wonder how a free nation ever allowed it. We question why our leaders let robber barons steal the wealth of all Americans for so many years until Teddy Roosevelt broke up the trusts. We recall images of Americans standing up to segregation who were mauled by attack dogs and lynched for seeking equality. We can feel pride that we finally elected someone of African lineage to the highest office in the land, but at the same time shame and dismay that a cadre with no respect for democracy replaced him.

But it's catching up. A Quinnipiac University poll released March 5, 2019 found 64 percent of Americans think Trump committed crimes before he became president and 24 percent say he did not. The same survey found 50 percent of those responding believed Michael Cohen's testimony in Congress late February, and 35 percent took Trump's side.

We've been through challenging times in the past. We overcame demagogues, and we can do it again. Wisconsin Senator Joseph McCarthy destroyed thousands of lives by falsely accusing people of disloyalty. His ruthless four-year campaign was so devastating that his name lives in infamy: tarnishing people with no evidence is appropriately called McCarthyism. His reign of terror ended suddenly during televised Senate hearings when the senator was accusing the U.S. Army of harboring Communists.

The Army's chief attorney, Joseph Welch, challenged McCarthy's "cruelty and recklessness" on June 9, 1954: "Let us not assassinate this lad further, senator. You have done enough. Have you no sense of decency, sir, at long last? Have you no sense of decency?"

Onlookers cheered Welch, and the nation was at long last relieved. The Senate later took the rare step of condemning McCarthy for "conduct contrary to senatorial traditions."

Democracy means nothing if it is not accompanied by decency. Who will be the Joseph Welch of the early twenty-first century and galvanize the nation by shaming Trump? When will someone with the stature of Welch ask Trump and the nation "Have you no sense of decency?"

APPENDIX A

Resources: Where to Go for Help

Believe nothing, no matter where you read it, or who said it,
no matter if I have said it, unless it agrees with your own reason
and your own common sense.

–Siddhartha Gautama (Buddha)

A CENTURY AGO, outrageous conspiracy theories were confined mainly to street corner crackpots shouting from soap boxes. A few, such as Father Charles Coughlin and Joseph McCarthy, managed to attract millions of followers. But by and large, conspiracists and demagogues got little attention by newspapers and radio broadcasts.

Nowadays, the Internet changed that. Both a curse and a blessing, it can provide instant information about illnesses, news from anywhere in any language, consumer goods, music, or a flight or cruise to anywhere in the world. But the downside is that it gives equal access to every conceivable kook, liar and swindler. Do we believe the Nigerian "prince" who wants to send us millions of dollars if we provide our banking information? No, we've learned to be skeptical. Then why believe other things that only take minutes to disprove?

APPENDIX A: WHERE TO GO FOR HELP

Sometimes it's hard to know what's true. Some websites offer help:

Abyznewslinks.com: A complete listing of newspapers and news websites around the world.

CJR.org: The *Columbia Journalism Review's* online site examines coverage of important news events for bias and accuracy.

FactCheck.org: Investigates claims by politicians and rates their veracity; it points out falsehoods and myths irrespective of political party or ideology. It has debunked a lot of Donald Trump's tall tales simply because he makes so many, but it is equally frank about false claims by Democrats.

Fair.org: The motto for Fairness and Accuracy in Reporting is "challenging media bias and censorship since 1986."

Journalism.org: Run by the Pew Research Center's Project for Excellence in Journalism, it examines media bias and provides relevant data about news content.

MediaMatters.org: Archives the worst of the worst misstatements made by politicians and news organizations, with links to audio and video. It was founded by former conservative hatchet man David Brock, who wrote *Blinded by the Right* and *The Republican Noise Machine*.

Newslink.org: A handy way to find websites for newspapers and broadcasters anywhere in the world.

Niemanlab.org: Nieman Journalism Lab is a project of the Nieman Foundation at Harvard University which describes itself as "a collaborative attempt to figure out how quality journalism can survive and thrive in the Internet age.

OpenSecrets.org: The nonpartisan Center for Responsive Politics exposes spending by organizations and affiliated groups to influence elections. Who is buying off your senator or member of Congress? They will tell you.

PolitiFact.com: Created by the *St. Petersburg Times* in Florida. It rates statements made by political leaders with its proprietary Truth-O-Meter, "a scorecard separating fact from fiction." It also investigates the memes making the rounds on influential blogs.

Poynter.net: Critiques the media and performs fact-checking.

ProPublica: An independent, nonprofit news organization with more than seventy-five journalists nationwide who vigorously pursue investigative journalism with the potential to spur impact. Their motto: "To expose abuses of power and betrayals of the public trust by government, business, and other institutions, using the moral force of investigative journalism to spur reform through the sustained spotlighting of wrongdoing."

Putintrump.org: A website operated by *Mother Jones* magazine which compiles news reports from many sources showing Trump's acquiescence to the Russian leader.

Rightwingwatch.org: Highlights extravagant claims made by right wingers. Entertaining but frightening.

Snopes.com: This highly respected website is devoted to debunking urban legends. It shows the sourcing for the information it provides so you can look it up yourself.

SourceWatch.org: A project of the Center for Media and Democracy is a media critic and also a Wikipedia-type reference about news sources. It exposes behind-the-scenes organizations and financing by big money groups messaging through mainstream media.

TruthorFiction.com: This website looks into rumors that have appeared on the Internet and judges their authenticity.

TyndallReport.com: Monitors broadcasts of the nightly network news (CBS, NBC and ABC). Andrew Tyndall claims to have not missed a single broadcast since 1987. The site compiles news reports on the frequency of coverage by network, trends in coverage and statistics.

Wikipedia.org: This volunteer-based website has had its share of goofs on occasion, but it strives for accuracy and is widely regarded for the amount of information it handles in a mostly evenhanded way. It tries to weed out incorrect and biased information. It scrupulously cites sources and deletes material considered biased.

APPENDIX B:
Bibliography/Recommended Books

A capacity, and taste, for reading gives access to
whatever has already been discovered by others

–Abraham Lincoln

T HERE MAY BE too many books already about Donald
Trump, but in my opinion, few are worthwhile. Here is
a list of the most compelling books which help readers
understand Trump and the environment, past and present,
which brought him to power.

For those seeking a bibliography, this is as close as you're
going to get. Quotations from any book or article published in
newspapers, magazines or websites are scrupulously cited so
readers can look them up easily. Broadcast quotes are cited by
media outlet and date if applicable. I would encourage readers
to look up the books on this list, because they are enlightening:

All the President's Men: Bob Woodward and Carl
Bernstein's 1974 account of uncovering Richard Nixon's
wrongdoing has stood the test of time and is particularly
relevant today when once again we confront a chief executive
who flouts the law. The story unwinds like a mystery novel as
the authors retrace the Watergate burglary by Nixon loyalists
through the steps that prompted his resignation. Readers also
get a front-row seat to the internal deliberations and ethical

dilemmas at *The Washington Post* on how the events were reported.

Dark Money: The Hidden History of the Billionaires Behind the Rise of the Radical Right: Jane Mayer's exposé was the first to trace the connections between the right-wing Koch Brothers and secretive moves to circumvent the will of the people with their desired outcomes. This is the best guide to understanding why our political system heavily favors a handful of big donors and ignores the rest of us. It's fair to say that Trump might not be president without the groundwork carefully laid by big-money right-wing groups.

Democracy in Chains: The Deep History of the Radical Right's Stealth Plan for America: Nancy McLean displays how little-known libertarian economist James McGill Buchanan managed to set the stage for a hostile takeover of our government and institutions. The author obtained exclusive access to Buchanan's personal papers which uncovered how he forged a working relationship with the Koch Brothers to reduce government regulations and promote privatization for the sole benefit of the wealthy.

Devil's Bargain: Focuses on Trump and campaign chief Steve Bannon, who previously ran Breitbart News, showing the dark side of the people behind Trump. Journalist Joshua Green lays bare how Trump and his handlers managed to exploit the far-right fringes and his television experience to take power.

Fear: Trump in the White House: Bob Woodward, *The Washington Post* editor who rocketed to prominence as a young reporter for exposing the Watergate scandal with Carl Bernstein, is a meticulous note taker and fact checker. Woodward reports that Trump is obsessed about the Russia investigation and that his advisers are often shocked by his lack of interest in and knowledge about major issues. The famous quote that then-Secretary of State Rex Tillerson called Trump a "moron," which was never denied, originated here. Another juicy bit of catnip for Trump critics was his quote of then-Defense Secretary James Mattis saying Trump understands military issues like a "fifth or sixth grader" while then-Chief of Staff John Kelly called Trump an "idiot" and described the White House staff as operating in "crazytown." Woodward wrote that former chief economic adviser Gary Cohn removed a draft letter he saw on Trump's desk that he considered dangerous for national security.

How Democracies Die: Steven Levitsky and Daniel Ziblatt , professors of government at Harvard University, have devoted their careers to analyzing how democracies descend into autocracy or outright dictatorship. They have focused mainly on Latin America, where many countries had democratic constitutions and institutions before coups or power grabs by strongmen on the left or right. They sound a loud warning that Trump has attempted to undermine the legitimacy of elections, baselessly describes opponents as criminals ("Lock Her Up"), encourages violence, and attempts to restrict basic civil liberties. Their research shows these phenomena to be precursors to totalitarianism.

Nineteen Eighty-Four: George Orwell's chilling futuristic dystopia opens with, "It was a bright cold day in April, and the clocks were striking thirteen," not unlike what many voters felt like on election night 2016. Citizens' lives are controlled by the Ministry of Truth, which invents its own truth, such as WAR IS PEACE, FREEDOM IS SLAVERY and IGNORANCE IS STRENGTH. The novel, published in 1949, suddenly became a best seller in early 2017 as Trump toadies described his lying as "alternative facts." If a politician or policy is described as "Orwellian," this novel is the reference point; "Big Brother" emerged from this story to describe a lack of privacy. Other modern classic novels now in vogue are Sinclair Lewis' *It Can't*

Happen Here about a demagogue who becomes U.S. president, published in 1935, and Aldous Huxley's *Brave New World* about a nightmarish futuristic society full of passive drones, published in 1932.

One Person, No Vote: If you are the least bit curious about all the rhetoric regarding voter fraud, this is the book for you. Carol Anderson researches the ploys used consistently by Republicans to prevent people from voting. If you are worried about what Trump is doing to America, this book proves unequivocally that he could have never been elected without the help of systematic voter suppression. Anderson draws a direct line between the Supreme Court's 2013 decision that eviscerated the Voting Rights Act and individual states using elaborate ruses to keep millions of people away from the polls. The author, a professor at Emory University, writes that politicians devise discriminatory rules "dressed up in the genteel garb of bringing 'integrity' to the voting booth."

Russian Roulette: The Inside Story of Putin's War on America and the Election of Donald Trump: Veteran investigative reporters David Corn and Michael Isikoff expose how Trump and Vladimir Putin have been collaborating for years, and how Trump is weakening NATO and the European Union to the benefit of Russia. The authors report extensively about contacts by Trump associates with Russians and point out that mainstream media devoted six times more space to Hillary Clinton's emails than to Trump's Russia connections. The book also explores why U.S. intelligence agencies did not do a better job of recognizing Russia's role in election meddling sooner and Barack Obama's failure to reveal more of what they knew before the election.

Team of Vipers: My 500 Extraordinary Days in the Trump White House: Cliff Sims, a former White House communications aide, writes a tell-all about vicious feuds and backstabbing in the West Wing, saying: "It's impossible to deny how absolutely out of control the White House staff – again, myself included – was at times." Sims describes a president suspicious of his own staff and describes John Kelly as confiding "this is the worst (expletive) job I've ever had." Sims confesses to have helped Trump compile his "enemies list," something no president since Nixon has done.

The Apprentice: Trump, Russia and the Subversion of American Democracy: Greg Miller, a *Washington Post* national security reporter and Pulitzer Prize winner, writes how Trump's slavishness toward Russia "occurred in plain sight," overwhelming the media's ability to keep up with it all. He shows how Trump exploits the divisions in American society "race, religion, guns and immigration" that Russia employed with its own social media meddling. Russian trolls infiltrated Facebook, Instagram, Twitter and YouTube to weaken Hillary Clinton after her condemnation of Russian elections' legitimacy. When Trump made divisive remarks, Miller writes, "Trump, again, was Putin's apprentice, summoning a side of America that sapped its claims to moral authority."

The Madhouse Effect: How Climate Change Denial is Threatening Our Planet, Destroying Our Politics, and Driving Us Crazy: Author Michael Mann, a professor of atmospheric science, punctures the myth-making machine and unmasks climate science deniers. Why is this book important? Because Trump said "the concept of global warming was created by and for the Chinese in order to make U.S. manufacturing noncompetitive." Mann makes it easy for the general public to understand the horrific dangers posed by global warming, to which none of us is immune. Since Trump pulled the nation out of the Paris Accords, sharing that ignominious distinction with only rogue states Syria and Nicaragua, it's vital that Americans demand to rejoin the world community on this serious issue that threatens us all. Tom Toles, a cartoonist at *The Washington*

Post, draws clever illustrations.

The Making of Donald Trump: Pulitzer Prize winner David Cay Johnston, who has written extensively about the economy and taxes, turns his sights on Trump's financial shenanigans and tax evasion. He discloses Trump's alleged connections to organized crime, cheating creditors and failing to pay his taxes. Johnston describes Trump as "a man with no moral core of any kind." His other book, *It's Even Worse Than You Think: What the Trump Administration is Doing to America,* describes Trump's mendacity and incompetence.

The Plot to Hack America: Malcolm Nance, with abundant street cred as an intelligence and foreign policy expert, brings a certain heft to his writing that other authors lack because instead of reporting about the topic, he knows it firsthand from the inside. Nance was way ahead of the curve: this book was published before the election. Instead of relying on anonymous sources, Nance draws on public records to connect the dots between Russia and election hacking. He describes Russian cyber warfare as "a melange of hostile cyber political and psychological operations in support of their national objectives, whether during peacetime or open war. It is now standard operating procedure." He quotes a former KGB officer as saying Russian intelligence targets "egocentric people who lack moral principles – who are either too greedy or who suffer from exaggerated self importance. These are the people the KGB wants and finds easiest to recruit." After seeing how many Trump associates have been prosecuted by Robert Mueller, that description should run cold chills up and down the spine of any patriotic American. Nance writes at the end of his book: "The Russian use of cyber weapons to perform criminal acts and damage our electoral process was intended to remove faith in America itself." By that measure, Putin's success exceeded his wildest expectations.

Trumpocracy: The Corruption of the American Republic:
Prominent conservative thinker David Frum makes the case
against Trump for grievous wounds against democracy as if he
were presenting the argument against the president for the Last
Judgment. "The government of the United States seems to have
made common cause with the planet's thugs, crooks, and
dictators against its own ideals – and in fact to have imported
the spirit of thuggery, crookedness, and dictatorship into the
very core of the American state, into the most solemn symbolic
oval center of its law and liberty," says the former speech writer
for George W. Bush. "He never understood that America's
power arose not only from its own wealth and its own military
force, but from its centrality to a network of friends and allies."
Frum asserts that Trump insists on flattery that Bush and other
presidents never allowed.

*Under Fire: Reporting from the Front Lines of the Trump
White House*: Trump called April Ryan, a black reporter for
American Urban Radio News, "nasty" and a "loser." That alone
would be reason to read her narrative. But Ryan sets the record
straight and proves how Trump's statements, especially
concerning race, are untrue. She gives a behind-the-scenes
glimpse at how others on the White House staff have treated
her as poorly as Trump did.

Unhinged: An Insider's Account of the Trump White House:
Former White House adviser Omarosa Manigault Newman,
who worked for Trump's television show, says she has a tape
recording of Trump using racist language. She also divulges
that the strategy of separating children from immigrant parents
was floated in the early days of the administration. And she
quotes Vice President Mike Pence's staff as saying they expect
Trump to not complete his term, which would elevate their boss
(whom they obsequiously call "the president") to the top spot.
Another slice of blistering trivia: Omarosa insists that Melania
plans to divorce Trump as soon as he leaves office.

APPENDIX C

Resources: Organizations That Need Your Help

Be the change that you wish to see in the world

–Mahatma Gandhi

MANY GROUPS working to guarantee democracy in the United States require citizen participation and/or donations. Some are nonpartisan, while several are liberal leaning and a couple of them are conservative. Here is a partial list of such groups, some a century old and others brand new:

AMERICAN CIVIL LIBERTIES UNION: Operating with the slogan "We the people dare to create a more perfect union," the ACLU formed in 1920 to protect individual rights when threatened. Among the founders were Helen Keller and Felix Frankfurter, later an associate justice on the Supreme Court. The group is not afraid to take unpopular stances such as demanding the right of Nazis to protest in Skokie, Illinois, a city with many Holocaust survivors. Since Trump took office, the ACLU fought his Muslim ban executive order and many other issues. The ACLU has traditionally brought together figures from the left and right with the common goal of fighting for the rights we all hold dear.

BRENNAN CENTER FOR JUSTICE: The center's stated goal: "The Brennan Center for Justice at NYU School of Law is a nonpartisan law and policy institute that works to reform, revitalize – and when necessary, defend – our country's systems of democracy and justice. At this critical moment, the Brennan Center is dedicated to protecting the rule of law and the values of constitutional democracy. We focus on voting rights, campaign finance reform, ending mass incarceration, and preserving our liberties while also maintaining our national security. Part think tank, part advocacy group, part cutting-edge communications hub, we start with rigorous research. We craft innovative policies. And we fight for them – in Congress and the states, the courts, and in the court of public opinion."

CHECKS & BALANCES: Formed by lawyers, including George Conway, a prominent Trump critic who is also the husband of White House counselor Kellyanne Conway. "We are a group of attorneys who would traditionally be considered conservative or libertarian. We believe in the rule of law, the power of truth, the independence of the criminal justice system, the imperative of individual rights, and the necessity of civil discourse. We believe these principles apply regardless of the party or persons in power. We believe in 'a government of laws, not of men.' We believe in the Constitution. We believe in free speech, a free press, separation of powers, and limited government. We have faith in the resiliency of the American experiment. We seek to provide a voice and a network for like-minded attorneys to discuss these ideas, and we hope that they will join with us to stand up for these principles." The group welcomes participation and donations from other barristers as well as non-lawyers.

COMMON CAUSE: With chapters in thirty-five states, this nonpartisan grassroots group is dedicated to upholding the core values of American democracy. It takes an active role in fighting partisan gerrymandering in redistricting nationwide and has filed lawsuits to fight the practice in several states.

DEFENDING DEMOCRACY TOGETHER INSTITUTE: Formed in 2018 by Bill Kristol, a prominent conservative who opposes Trump. The group is fighting to "counter popular misconceptions about immigrants, especially Hispanic immigrants," works to protect the Mueller investigation from political interference, opposes tariffs, and resists Trump's unwillingness to stand up to Vladimir Putin. Its website has an analysis of Russian interference in U.S. politics.

EMERGE AMERICA: Recruits, trains and supports women running for office nationwide, having trained more than two-thousand five-hundred women to date. It says that 415 of its alumnae on the ballot won their elections in 2018.

EMILY'S LIST: The largest organization promoting Democratic women in politics. The name originated as an acronym for "Early Money Is Like Yeast." It claims to have helped elect more than a hundred women to the U.S. House, twenty-three to the Senate, twelve to governorships and hundreds to state legislatures.

FLIPPABLE: "Our democracy is upside-down. At Flippable, we believe in creating a government for the people. That's why we focus on states, where the rules of the country's democracy are written. Our community supports progressive candidates – and flips strategic states blue. Together, we're building good government from the ground level up!" The group raised $2.1 million for candidates in the 2018 midterm elections, supporting eighty-one candidates who won elections as well as helping flip five state chambers.

INDIVISIBLE: A movement of progressives working against the Trump agenda. Founders modeled it as the mirror opposite of the Tea Party, which opposed Barack Obama's agenda to bail out the economy when we were hurtling toward another Great Depression. Indivisible fought Republican efforts in Congress to destroy the Affordable Care Act (Obamacare), demonstrated against Trump's Cabinet nominees with conflicts of interest and encouraged people to make their voices heard at town hall meetings.

LEAGUE OF WOMEN VOTERS: "Committed to making democracy work for voters through programs of promoting voter registration, working to reduce the influence of large-donor money in political campaigns, and seeking to reform political gerrymandering that favors one party over the other or protects incumbent office holders."

OPERATION 45: "A group of Freedom of Information Act (FOIA) legal experts and activists working to keep President Trump's (45) administration transparent and accountable to the people it serves."

PEOPLE FOR THE AMERICAN WAY: "People For the American Way and its affiliate, People For the American Way Foundation, are progressive advocacy organizations founded to fight right-wing extremism and defend constitutional values under attack, including free expression, religious liberty, equal justice under the law, and the right to meaningfully participate in our democracy."

PUBLIC CITIZEN: Founded by consumer advocate Ralph Nader in 1971, this organization "champions the public interest" in the halls of power. "We have defended democracy, resisted corporate power and worked to ensure that government works for the people – not for big corporations." It claims to have four hundred thousand members. "We do not participate in partisan political activities or endorse any candidates for elected office." Public Citizen is a leader in highlighting Trump's conflicts of interest.

APPENDIX C: ORGANIZATIONS THAT NEED YOUR HELP

SHE SHOULD RUN: "Women are under-represented at all levels of government from local school board races to the White House. She Should Run was founded in 2011 to address this very problem." The group encourages women to run for public office if they have been nominated by a member.

SISTER DISTRICT PROJECT: The group "works to ensure that all Americans have equal representation and our government works for all people, not just the minority in power." It is "open to volunteers and candidates of all genders," focusing on local elections to flip Republican legislatures, preserve Democratic majorities in states where they exist, and work against gerrymandering and voter suppression.

SWING LEFT: During the 2018 midterm elections it made 2.5 million phone calls, knocked on five million doors and raised ten million dollars for Democratic candidates in swing districts. The group is now devoted to swing seats in the Senate and House as well as state legislatures in 2020 to guarantee "fair maps in the 2021 redistricting."

INDEX

INDEX

INDEX

INDEX

ABOUT THE AUTHOR

JOHN WRIGHT was born in Flint, Michigan and moved to the West Coast when he was eight. A resident of Seattle, he has previously lived in California, Oregon, Hawaii, Wyoming, New York, Venezuela, Mexico and Brazil.

He graduated from Humboldt State University in Northern California and later studied at New York University and graduate school at the University of Washington. He has worked as a journalist at community newspapers in Wyoming and Seattle; the English-language *Daily Journal* in Caracas, Venezuela; The Associated Press; Dow Jones & Company; Knight Ridder Financial/Bridge News and Energy News Today.

His previous books are: *The Obama Haters: Behind the Right-Wing Campaign of Lies, Innuendo & Racism* (Potomac Books, 2011); *Life Without Oil: Why We Must Shift to a New Energy Future* (co-author with Steve Hallett, Prometheus Books, 2011), *Lost & Found in Latin America: All About Brazil's World Cup Soccer, the Argentine Pope & Mariachi* (Rainy City Publishing, 2014).